Cooking With Wine

by

Virginia and Robert Hoffman

Authors of:
The California Wine Country Cookbook, I & II
The California Wine Country Herbs & Spices Cookbook
The Great Little Food With Wine Cookbook
The Great Turkey Cookbook
The Great Chicken Cookbook
The Holidays Cookbook
Salsas!

The Hoffman Press
Santa Rosa, California

Cover Illustration: "Autumn Vineyard" by Ellie Marshall
Drawings from "The Spice Cookbook," © 1964, 1991. All rights reserved. Published by David White Company, Willsboro, NY 12996. Used with permission.

Typeset by Nancy LaMothe

Quantity discounts and bulk purchases of this and other Hoffman Press books are available. Call or fax the National Sales Manager at (707) 538-5527, Fax 538-7371. Printed in the United States of America.

Publisher's Cataloging-in-Publication
(Provided by Quality Books, Inc.)

Hoffman, Virginia M.
        Cooking with wine : 172 cooking with wine recipes : pairing food with wine : the varietal wines of America / by Virginia and Robert Hoffman.
    p. cm.
    Includes index.
    ISBN 0-9629927-3-9
    1. Cookery (Wine) I. Hoffman, Robert P. II. Title
TX726.H64 1997   641.6'22
                                QBI97-40459

CONTRIBUTORS

We want to acknowledge the help that we have received in writing this book. We are indebted to two people who contribute substantially to our books: Nancy LaMothe, who structures our recipes (this is her ninth book with us), and Ellie Marshall, the distinguished artist who illustrates our covers.

We want to thank the wineries, large and small, throughout the United States, who responded to our request for "Your best recipes using wine as an important ingredient". Their submissions were, as evidenced by many of the recipes in this book, highly creative. We think you will enjoy making them as much as we did.

Recipe Contributors*

Adelsheim Winery, Adler Fels Winery, Alderbrook Vineyards, Arbor Crest Winery, Arrowood Vineyards & Winery, Audobon Cellars, Beaucanon Winery, Benziger Family Winery, Beringer Vineyards, Brotherhood Winery, Buena Vista Winery, Carneros Estate, Cakebread Cellars, Canandaigua Wine Co., Carneros Alambic Distillery, Charles Spinetta Winery, Chateau St. Jean, Chateau Ste. Michelle, Chateau Elan, Ltd., Chrlstopher Creek Winery, Columbia Wines, Concannon Vineyard, Cordoniu Napa, De Loach Vineyards, Domaine Carneros, Domaine Cheurlin, Duckhorn Vineyards, Domaine Chandon, Dry Creek Vineyards, Dunnewood Vineyards and Winery.

Edgewood Estate, Fess Parker Winery, Ferrari-Carano Winery, Franciscan Oakville Estate, Freemark Abbey, Freixenet Sonoma Champagne Caves, Glen Ellen Vineyards & Winery, Heron Hill Vineyards, Heublein Inc., Hogue Cellars.

Kendall-Jackson Vineyards, Kenwood Vineyards, Korbel Champagne Cellars, Kunde Estate, Laurel Ridge Winery, Landmark Vineyards, Louis M. Martini, J. Lohr Winery & Vineyards, Martinl & Prati Winery, Mark West Vineyards, Markham Winery, Matanzas Creek Winery, Merryvale Vineyards, Mirassou, Monterey Vineyards, Mumm Napa, Murphy Goode Estate Winery.

III

Contributors

Navarro Winery, Peju Province, J. Pedroncelli Winery, Piper Sonoma, Quivera Vineyards, Ravenswood, Raymond Vineyard & Cellar, Robert Mondavi Winery, Rutherford Hill Winery.

V. Sattui Winery, Ste. Chapelle Winery, Inc., St. Julian Wine Co, Inc., Sausal Winery, Simi Winery, Inc., Scharffenberger Cellars, Smothers Bros. Winery, Sokol Blesser Winery, Stag's Leap Cellars, St. Supery Vineyards & Winery, St. Francis Winery, Sterling Vineyards, Stone Hill Wine Co., Sutter Home Winery, Taylor Wine Co., Tomasello Winery, Inc., Viansa Winery, Whitehall Lane Winery, Windsor Winery.

*A note regarding the recipes:

All of them were reformatted from the original to provide the reader with the ingredients and the instructions in the order in which they are used. In some cases where ingredients were local and not available nationally, we have substituted equivalent ingredients that are found in most supermarkets, gourmet grocery stores, or from major mail order firms.

Many of the recipe names have been changed from the original due to duplication or similarity of names. We have not attributed specific recipes to specific wineries because there was considerable duplication. But they're all good. They've all been tested and they'll give you, your family and your guests, delightful culinary experiences!

TABLE OF CONTENTS

PREFACE

Ever wonder why a particular dish in a restaurant or in someone else's home tastes so much better than when you make it?

The answer is probably in the fact that wine was used as an ingredient. Wine imparts a certain bringing-together of flavors, first by blending them, and then by sharpening or strengthening them. Nothing has ever been found that equals wine in cooking. If you have never cooked with wine, you have some wonderful cooking experiences ahead!

Before getting into which wine goes into which food, let's clarify a couple of things.

First, you *can't* cook well with bad wine. This does not mean you cannot use inexpensive wines. It simply means that if it tastes vinegary, raw, or unpleasant, throw it out. You are wasting time and money by trying to cook with bad wine. If you think that cooking with it will smooth it out or that it won't make a difference because there are so many other ingredients, you are wrong. A small amount of bad wine can ruin a dish, just as one rotten apple can spoil a barrelful.

Second, *when* you add the wine to the other ingredients is crucial. Don't make the mistake of adding it too soon, or too late. Wine performs in certain ways in certain conditions. For example, a beef stew will usually call for the wine to be added early in the recipe so it can marinate the meat, blend the other spices, and evaporate the alcohol during cooking.

A soup such as a shrimp bisque will have the wine added just before it is served to provide the whole flavor of the wine, which would be dispelled if cooked. So be meticulous in adding the wine when the recipe calls for it.

Third, one of the old "rules" of cooking with wine said you should cook with the same wine that you are going to drink with the dish. This is not only absurd, it is also stupid.

If, for example, you have a cherished thirty year old bottle of Burgundy, don't cook with it. The cooking will remove all the fine nuances of flavor that make it so valuable. Use a good Burgundy for your cooking and serve the vintage Burgundy to accompany it. This is true of any wine, so save the really, really fine wines for drinking and use a good quality wine of the same varietal for cooking.

Fourth, after you are familiar with which wines you enjoy cooking and serving, *experiment*! If the recipe calls for Gewürztraminer try a Sémillon, White Zinfandel or another white wine. If you really prefer red wines, *experiment*! Try a recipe that specifies a white wine, with a red wine. That's how most recipes are created — by trying different ingredients. Some are just great and we remember them. Others we chalk up to experience and forget.

Fifth, enjoy yourself! We do, and we hope that with this book you will, too. Cooking with wine is a joyous adventure.

Virginia and Robert Hoffman

COOKING WITH WINE CAN BE GOOD FOR YOUR HEALTH

You can drastically reduce the amount of calories, sodium, fat and cholesterol when you cook with wine. Here's how:

Wine adds a richness to foods that easily replaces high calorie ingredients. Using dessert as an example, fruit which is poached in wine, and is served with a cookie or two is less than half the calories of a slice of chocolate cake.

Another example is the substitution of a sorbet (such as the Champagne Sorbet in this book), in place of ice cream. Compare its ingredients of sugar, water, fruit flavor and Champagne with those for ice cream which include eggs, cream, milk and sugar.

You'll use less salt, too, when you cook with wine. Salt is replaced by the rich nuances of flavor of the ingredients in the dish, when combined with wine, and thus lessens the need for salt to enhance these flavors. A beef stew made with a hearty burgundy, for example, really doesn't need more than a pinch of salt.

We suggest that you resist the temptation to add salt to any dish in which wine is an important ingredient. If more salt is required, you may add it just before serving; or, better yet, allow the diner to determine if the dish needs salt.

In poaching fish in white wine, for example, we have found that the wine brings out the essences of the herbs and spices that we have in the recipe far better than when salt is used.

One further point: salt has a tendency to toughen meat, fish and poultry, while wine tenderizes in the marinating process.

When cooking with wine, you can drastically reduce the amount of fats and oil that you use very simply. In place of your usual butter, margarine or cooking oil use a few drops of olive oil or a spray or two of a cooking oil to cook meat, poultry or fish. Follow by liberal usage of wine to complete the cooking by poaching instead of frying.

5

Broiling a steak in an oven or on a barbeque is a good example. A light coating of olive oil on the steak, just enough to prevent its sticking to the grill or pan surface, followed by a quarter cup of a hearty red wine such as a Barbera, Beaujolais, or Merlot brushed or poured over the meat, will provide you with a whole new dimension in the flavor of the steak.

If panfried, the wine along with the brown bits in the pan stirred together with a little flour will give you a sauce that is a true gourmet's delight, with the fat and calorie count greatly reduced.

Cholesterol levels, too, are greatly decreased as wine is used in place of cheese, cream, butter and fat. The natural goodness of your dish is enhanced, and high cholesterol sauces of these products are not necessary to achieve great dishes when you cook with wine.

Besides being good for your health, cooking with wine opens new doors to dishes that you have created using the wines of your choice.

Pairing these dishes with wines to complement them is probably the most rewarding of all culinary achievements, and it is not at all difficult to achieve.

It's nice to know that it is possible to eat well, drink well and enjoy better nutrition, too, isn't it?

The Varietal
Wines of
North America

COOKING WITH WINE

THE VARIETAL WINES OF NORTH AMERICA

Selecting wine by the varietal of the grapes from which it was made is becoming the most popular (and easiest) way to select a wine. This is due to the proliferation of brand names and proprietary labels as winemakers seek to establish a market for their specific brand name. Because every wine label must identify the varietal of grapes, this is your easiest way to select wines: by the grapes from which it was made.

There are wide differences in the making of wine from grapes, even though they may be all made from the same varietal of grapes. Climate and soil are important factors, as are the quality of the grapes. Of equal or sometimes greater importance is the skill of the winemaker in the conversion of grapes to wine.

These descriptions of the most popular wines made in North America will give you an indication of the taste of the wine, from which you can make your own determination as to the varietal you like. From that you can try various brand names within those categories to determine which you want to buy.

The best way to buy wine is to taste it. Many wine shops have tastings. There are now wine bars in many states. The method we suggest is to visit wineries. Your next vacation can include a day or two of visiting wineries, tasting wines, and buying the wines that you have watched being made.

THE WHITE WINES

Chardonnay is the most popular white wine, probably because it is compatible with so many different foods. Poultry, fish, pork, and even beef go well with Chardonnay. Its rich buttery taste makes it the "safe" choice. If you don't know what to serve, serve a Chardonnay.

Chenin Blanc is usually either very dry or sweet. The eastern part of America seems to prefer the sweet, while the western states buy the dry. A good light white wine, the sweet versions go well with light summer foods such as chicken, salads and seafood, and the dry versions are good year round with poultry and seafood.

Columbard, which is sometimes labeled French Columbard, has a delightful, fruity taste. It is particularly good when served well chilled with summer picnics and informal dinners, such as barbecues.

Gewürztraminer has become very popular, thanks to its spicy characteristics. It is produced in many degrees of taste, ranging from very dry to very sweet. The very driest goes well with most foods, particularly chicken and broiled fish, and the sweeter ones with salads and soup. The very sweetest is a "Late Harvest," which is a dessert wine.

Moscato Canelli is a sweet, heavy dessert wine with a very definite raisin flavor. A personal favorite of ours is to use it as a sauce with rice or bread pudding.

Muller-Thurgau is a unique wine, in that it's a cross of the Reisling and Sylvaner grape stocks to produce grapes that can be grown in cold climates. Widely grown in the Pacific Northwest and Canada, it has a slightly sweet taste.

Niagara, like a Muller-Thurgau, is grown mostly in colder climates. It is widely grown in the Finger Lakes District of New York, and in Arkansas, Michigan, Missouri, Pennsylvania and Canada. Slightly sweet in flavor, it goes well with stews, pot roasts, and casseroles.

Pinot Blanc, a close relative to Chardonnay, has slightly less intensity in flavor than Chardonnay. It goes well with most foods, as does Chardonnay, and is also a "safe choice" to serve with practically any meal featuring poultry, seafood, or pork.

Pinot Gris is also known as Pinot Grigio or Tokày. This wine is full-bodied with spicy overtones, and goes well with many foods. Because of its full-body and heaviness, it is best not to serve it with light foods, particularly cream sauces. It is, however, ideal for bolder-flavored foods, such as barbecued or grilled poultry and fish.

Reisling, which is also known as Johannisberg Reisling, has a great range of flavors from very dry to sweet. This classic white wine, popular in Europe for centuries, is now being made in the United States and in Canada. It is a great wine for summer dining, or as a well-chilled summer drink. You may be familiar with a very popular Eastern summer drink called "A Reisling Spritz," which is Reisling wine, ice cubes and a spritz or splash of soda.

Sauvignon Blanc is a classic French wine, that is now being made here. The dryer versions are often called Fumé Blanc. Like Chardonnay and Pinot Blanc, it goes well with most foods, and is also a "safe choice".

Sémillon is a light wine, and is usually quite dry. It is particularly good with light foods, such as broiled chicken and fish. It is growing in popularity because of its distinctive fresh fruity flavor.

THE RED WINES

Barbera, which originated in Italy, is now vinted in the United States, principally in California. Like Nebbiolo and Sangovese, it has a rich, sharp clean taste that is a perfect accompaniment to most Italian dishes. It is also very, very good with barbecued pork or beef.

Beaujolais (also known as Gamay and Napa Beaujolais) is not really a Beaujolais, but a relative of Pinot Noir. It is believed to have gotten its name from the method of making the wine, which is very similar to that used for Beaujolais wine. It is a fragrant light wine, particularly good with light summer meals.

Cabernet Sauvignon is the classic red wine of France, and is now being grown and vinted extensively in the United States in such diverse locations as central California and the suburbs of New York City on Long Island. Its rich, intense flavors of cassis and raspberry complement any beef dish, although many (including one of the editors of this book) have it with cold-water ocean fish such as tuna, halibut, and salmon.

Cabernet Franc is very similar to Cabernet Sauvignon, and was originally used only for blending. Recently, it has built a reputation of its own as a lighter version of Cabernet Sauvignon. It is well-suited to the same dishes as a Cabernet Sauvignon.

Catawba is a native American! First discovered in North Carolina, its grapes are used to make the inexpensive white and sparkling wines that are popular on the East Coast.

Concord grapes are best known as the source for grape juice, and for grape jams and jellies. This is the second largest varietal of grapes grown in the United States. It is grown throughout the eastern States and Canada. It is used in making, and/or blending with, a wide variety of red wines

Grenache is the grape from which most blush, pink, or rosé wines were made in the United States until Zinfandel grapes were introduced here. It is the base of many commercial wines such as those termed "Jug" wines. Grown mostly in California and Oregon, it is one of the least expensive. Grenache goes well with most light foods. Serve it well chilled.

Mission Grapes are included purely for their historical reference. They were originally brought to California from Mexico in the 1700s by Father Junipero Serra and his Franciscan missionaries, and became the foundation of the entire California wine industry.

Merlot is rapidly becoming one of the most popular red wines in the United States and Canada. It is similar to Cabernet Sauvignon, but is somewhat mellower and softer to the taste. Merlot is well suited for practically all meat dishes, and pairs well with cold-water fish.

Petite Syrah, also known as Petit Syrah, Petite Sirah, and Petit Sirah, is robust and full-bodied with peppery overtones. While it is widely used as a blending grape to add body and character to other red wines, it is an ideal accompaniment to many meat dishes.

Pinot Noir is now becoming one of the more popular wines here, since growers have moved their vineyards to cooler climates such as Northern California, Oregon and Central California. Its Burgundy-like flavor is well suited to any dish calling for a rich, spicy, full-bodied wine.

Zinfandel grapes are made into such a wide range of tastes, that it is almost impossible to categorize them. They can range in flavor from a very light wine like a Grenache, to a rich, full-bodied wine like a Cabernet Sauvignon. White Zinfandel and Blush Zinfandels have become so popular that thousands of acres are being planted to meet the demand. Requiring a special label because of its unique characteristics is "Late Harvest Zinfandel," that is ideal for serving with desserts or in place of Port.

MISCELLANEOUS
Although these are not based on varietals, we have included them.

Champagne and Sparkling Wine are made from several different varietals, in both reds and whites. There is considerable confusion in the use of the term "Champagne" and "Sparkling Wine". In theory, wines made by the methode champenoise of fermenting in the bottle in the Champagne region of France are the only Champagne bottles that may bear that label in Europe.

But, here in the United States, the Charmat or tank-fermented wines are also often labeled Champagne, although the purists insist that they should be called "Sparkling Wine". To further add to the confusion, many Champagnes or Sparkling Wines in the United States are owned by French firms, who make their Champagne (Sparkling Wine) in the classic methode champenoise method, but prefer to call their product "Sparkling Wine" to protect their French products also marketed in the United States.

There are several degrees of sweetness in this wine. The driest is labeled "Extra Brut". The next is "Brut" (the most popular). "Extra Dry" isn't -- it's medium dry. "Sec" is slightly sweet, and "Demi-Sec" is quite sweet. The sweetest of all is "Doux".

Brandy is distilled from mostly white grapes, and is not wine because it contains more than 14% alcohol. When you cook with it, use very little, as it has a strong flavor. Use it for finishing cooked meat or poultry, and for last minute flavoring of desserts.

Port is distilled from red grapes, and like Sherry is a fortified wine. Quite sweet, it is customarily served after a meal. It is also good for simmering fruits, and for adding to mincemeat pie.

Sherry, another fortified wine, originated in Spain. It is made in a wide range of flavors, quality, and sweetness. "Finos" are light and dry. "Manzanillas" are very light, very dry and have a hint of salt. "Amontillados" are softer, sweeter and darker than the Finos. "Oloroso" is the most fully flavored, is quite dark in color, and is aged the longest. Sherry is also known as Cream Sherry or Golden Sherry. It is ideal for preparing sauces for seafood, and for adding flavor to mushroom soup, crab or shrimp bisques, or tomato soup just before serving.

Vermouth is a white wine that has been fortified and flavored with herbs and spices. There are two versions: "Dry Vermouth" and "Sweet Vermouth". Dry Vermouth is served as an aperitif or as an appetizer. It is well suited for cooking mushrooms, chicken, fish, and pork. "Sweet Vermouth" is ideal for beef stews, marinating steaks and chops, and in barbequing.

Appetizers &
Light Foods

COOKING WITH WINE

New Orleans Shrimp & Chicken Creole, with Cornbread Toast

½ cup chicken stock
½ cup finely chopped red bell
  pepper
½ cup minced green bell
  pepper
1 cup finely chopped scallions
½ cup finely chopped celery
3 cloves fresh garlic, minced
2 cups canned crushed
  tomatoes
½ cup Merlot wine
2 tablespoons tomato paste
2 tablespoons red wine
  vinegar
½ teaspoon dried thyme
  leaves

¼ teaspoon mace
¼ teaspoon allspice
1 teaspoon chile powder
1 bay leaf
¼ teaspoon salt
1 cup chopped fresh okra, cut
  into ½-inch pieces
½ pound chicken breasts, cut
  into ½ -inch julienne strips
3 ounces pepperoni, cut into
  ⅛-inch thick slices and
  halved
½ pound medium shrimp,
  peeled
6 large corn muffins, split and
  toasted

Heat stock in large enameled pan over medium heat. Add peppers, scallions, celery and garlic. Cook for 10 minutes.

Add tomatoes, wine, tomato paste, vinegar, herbs and spices. Bring to a boil, lower heat and simmer 10 minutes. Add okra and cook 5 minutes. Then add the chicken breasts and cook about 20 minutes. Add pepperoni and shrimp, cooking for 3 minutes until shrimp are done. Remove bay leaf.

To serve, put 2 halves of corn muffin on each plate, toasted side up. Cover with 1 ½ cups of shrimp chicken creole. Makes 6 servings.

Serve with a Merlot or Cabernet Sauvignon.

Ham à la King in Pastry Shells

1 red bell pepper, chopped
1 small onion, minced
1 pound ham, diced
2 tablespoons butter or
  margarine
2 tablespoons flour
1 ½ cups milk, at room
  temperature

2 cups shredded sharp
  Cheddar cheese
¾ cup Chardonnay wine or
  Sherry
1 cup frozen petite peas
6 prepared individual pastry
  shells, baked according to
  package directions

On low heat, sauté the pepper, onion and ham until tender. Set aside.

In a saucepan, make the cheese sauce by slowly melting the butter. After it is melted, add the flour 1 tablespoon at a time, stirring constantly. Add the milk slowly, and continue stirring. Then, slowly add the cheese. Still stirring constantly, add the wine or Sherry. Cook over low heat until it bubbles. Add the meat and vegetables.

Pour into the prepared pastry shells.   Serves 6.

Serve with a Chardonnay or Pinot Blanc.

Shredded Duck Crepes with Champagne Sauce

1 whole duck	12 crepes
2 cups Champagne	1 cup cooked white beans
2 tablespoons chopped garlic	⅓ cup orange zest
2 cups heavy cream	⅓ cup Brandy
2 tablespoons chopped parsley	1 teaspoon thyme
Salt and pepper	Butter for sauté

In a large pot cover duck with water. Add one chopped carrot, onion and celery. Boil for two hours. Remove duck from stock. Let cool enough to handle. Remove skin and bones from duck and return them to stock. Simmer for one hour. Meanwhile shred duck meat and set aside. Strain duck stock.

Return 3 cups of the duck stock to the heat, adding the Champagne and garlic. Reduce by half. Add the heavy cream. Continue reducing to desired thickness (about ½ hour). Remove from heat and add parsley and salt and pepper to taste.

Lay out crepes onto work surface. In a mixing bowl combine shredded duck, white beans, orange zest, Brandy, thyme and salt and pepper. Fill the center of crepes with 2 tablespoons of duck mixture. Fold two sides in and two sides together. Heat one tablespoon butter in sauté pan and cook crepes till golden brown. Warm sauce and transfer crepes to plate. Ladle sauce over crepes and garnish with Golden Raspberry Salsa. Serves 6.

GOLDEN RASPBERRY SALSA:

1 pint golden raspberries	2 tablespoons lime juice
¼ cup finely diced red onion	Salt
2 tablespoons orange juice	2 tablespoons chopped
¼ cup finely diced yellow bell	cilantro
pepper	1 jalapeno, finely diced

Combine all ingredients until well mixed.

Serve with a Champagne (Brut).

Cheese Log with Sun-Dried Tomatoes

8 ounces cream cheese, softened

¾ cup chopped oil-packed sun-dried tomatoes

¼ cup (or about 10) chopped kalamata olives

2 tablespoons chopped fresh basil

2 tablespoons chopped pine nuts

2 tablespoons chopped chives

2 tablespoons chopped arugula

1 medium clove garlic, minced

2 tablespoons grated Parmesan cheese

2 tablespoons Sauvignon Blanc, or other white wine

½ cup whole pine nuts for garnish

Spread softened cream cheese about ¼-inch thick on a 7 × 9-inch piece of plastic wrap. (This is a little easier if you use both a spatula and clean, water-moistened fingers.) Chill the cheese while chopping the other ingredients. Mix the next nine ingredients together. Spread the mixture onto the chilled cream cheese to about ¼ inch from all edges, pressing down a bit so that it makes a compact layer.

Loosen one of the short ends from the plastic wrap with a spatula. By lifting the end of the plastic wrap, start to roll tightly so that it sticks together and has a swirl of cheese in the middle (but not so tightly that you squash it). Keep pulling the plastic wrap away as you roll. You will end up with a very neatly wrapped cheese log which you can make ahead of time and refrigerate.

Before serving press whole pine nuts on top for decoration. Serve with bread or crackers.   Serves 6.

Serve with any dry white wine.

Smoked Salmon Filled Puffs

PUFF SHELLS* - (Pâte à choux):

¾ cup water	4 ounces butter
¼ cup milk	1 ¼ cups bread flour
¼ teaspoon salt	4 eggs

Preheat the oven to 375 degrees.

Combine water, milk, salt and butter in saucepan. Bring to a rolling boil. Add flour all at once and beat until mixture leaves sides of pan and starts to coat bottom of pan. Remove from heat. Let cool slightly, then beat in eggs one at a time. Drop rounded teaspoonful of batter onto greased cookie sheet and bake approximately 15 to 20 minutes, or until puffs are quite brown and very firm. Once cooled, cut tops off puffs; reserve for garnish.

SMOKED SALMON AND CHEESE FILLING:

REDUCTION:

½ cup puréed shallots	1 ½ cups Chardonnay wine
2 tablespoons butter	¾ cup heavy cream

Sauté shallots in butter until soft. Add wine and reduce by half. Add ¾ cup cream and reduce by half again. Cool slightly.

FILLING:

1 cup of above reduction	¼ cup finely chopped green onions
3 ounces Gorgonzola cheese	
3 ounces cream cheese	Salt and white pepper
1 cup finely chopped smoked salmon	Fresh dill for garnish

Thoroughly mix the reduction, cheeses, salmon and onion. Season to taste with salt and pepper. Fill puff shells. Garnish with a sprig of fresh dill and place the reserved tops on the puffs.

Makes 40 to 50 puffs.

*Small puff shells can be purchased ready-made in supermarkets.

Serve with a Chardonnay, Pinot Blanc or Champagne (Brut).

Mushrooms in Garlic Sauce

6 tablespoons butter, at room
  temperature
1 tablespoon minced garlic
1 ½ pounds mushrooms,
  cleaned and stemmed

1 ½ cups Champagne (Brut)
Salt and pepper
1 to 2 tablespoons minced
  fresh parsley or mixed fresh
  herbs

In a 10-inch skillet, melt 3 tablespoons of the butter over medium heat; add garlic. Cook and stir garlic until lightly browned; add mushrooms. Cook, stirring occasionally, until lightly browned, about 5 minutes. Add Champagne; bring to boil. Reduce heat; simmer until liquid is reduced to ⅓ cup, about 10 minutes. Taste and adjust seasoning with salt and pepper.

Remove from heat and whisk in remaining butter, bit by bit, until sauce is slightly thickened. Arrange mushrooms in serving dish with toothpick inserted in each. Pour sauce over; garnish with minced parsley or fresh herbs.   Serves 6.

Serve with a Champagne (Brut).

Chicken Breast & Prosciutto Spread

2 onions, chopped
2 celery stalks, chopped
2 carrots, chopped
1 tablespoon butter
6 double chicken breasts,
  cubed
1 ½ pounds ground pork
2 ¼ pounds softened butter,
  cut into 9 cubes

1 cup Brandy
3 teaspoons salt
3 teaspoons tarragon
3 dashes Tabasco
¾ teaspoon quatre épices*
¾ teaspoon white pepper
1 cup cubed prosciutto or
  smoked ham

Sauté the onions, celery and carrots in 1 tablespoon of the butter until soft. Add the chicken and pork; sauté until tender and cooked through, 10 to 15 minutes. Drain and cool slightly.

Working with ⅓ at a time, process the meat mixture in a food processor until smooth. Add ⅓ of the softened butter, ⅓ of the Brandy and ⅓ of seasonings and mix until blended. Pour into bowl and repeat twice more. Stir all together to mix batches. Fold in cubed prosciutto and pack into loaf pans or crocks. Serve with crusty French bread slices.   Makes two 3-pound loaves.

*Quatre épices (4 spices), a blend of white pepper, cloves, nutmeg and ground ginger, is often used in pâtes. You can find it in most supermarkets.

Serve with Chardonnay or a dry Zinfandel.

Smoked Duck Crepes
with Blood Orange Beurre Blanc

1 whole smoked duck (or roast duck if smoked is not available)	5 whole white peppercorns
	15 pink peppercorns, slightly crushed
6 blood oranges	1 sprig of thyme
8 shallots	1 cup Champagne (Brut)
2 teaspoons olive oil	2 tablespoons wine vinegar
2 cubes plus 2 tablespoons unsalted butter	1 ½ tablespoons heavy cream
	Salt and white pepper
¼ cup finely chopped basil	Savory Crepes (recipe follows)

Shred duck meat off of bones, removing any excess fat. Peel and segment three of the blood oranges, and squeeze the remaining three for juice. Set aside.

Peel and quarter seven of the eight shallots. Using an oven-proof skillet, sauté the quartered shallots in olive oil and place in a 350 degree oven until well caramelized. Remove from oven.

Melt 2 tablespoons of the butter in a saucepan. Heat the duck in the butter and add the caramelized shallots and the basil.

To make the beurre blanc, peel and finely mince the remaining shallot. Place the blood orange juice in a small saucepan and reduce to ¼ cup.

In a separate saucepan, place the minced shallot, both types of peppercorns, thyme, Champagne and vinegar. Reduce liquid to 3 to 4 tablespoons. Turn heat to low and whisk the two cubes of butter one tablespoon at a time into the reduced liquid. (Take care to whisk the butter continually as it melts and incorporates; allowing the butter to melt without whisking will cause the sauce to break.) When all of the butter is incorporated, whisk in the blood orange reduction and the cream. Season to taste with salt and pepper.

Add ¼ cup of the beurre blanc to the duck mixture and combine. ·Add the blood orange segments and mix gently.

SAVORY CREPES:

1 cup water	¼ teaspoon salt
1 cup milk	3 tablespoons unsalted butter,
4 eggs, large	melted
2 cups all-purpose flour	

Blend water, milk and eggs together with a whisk or in a blender. Slowly add flour and salt; continue to whisk or blend until smooth . Blend in melted butter and refrigerate for at least 30 minutes. The batter should be the consistency of heavy cream. If the batter is too thick, add a little water.

Heat a crepe pan (or a 6 or 8-inch non-stick sauté pan) over moderate heat. Brush with a little clarified butter or oil. The pan is hot enough when a drop of batter sizzles on the pan. While rolling the pan around, add ¼ cup of the batter making a thin layer that covers the bottom of the pan.

Cook until the sides of the crepe turn light brown and lift slightly from the surface of the pan. Flip using a thin rubber spatula and cook other side until brown. Remove and repeat the cooking process until batter is used up. Makes about 12 crepes.

Roll the finished filling mixture into Savory Crepes. Top with beurre blanc and garnish with basil sprigs. Serves 6.

Serve with Champagne (Brut).

Smoked Trout Mousse

½ pound smoked trout, skinned and boned (about 2 fish)
¼ cup mayonnaise
Juice of one lemon
1 to 2 tablespoons horseradish

2 tablespoons Fumé Blanc wine
1 pound cream cheese, softened
Black pepper

Put all ingredients in a food processor. Process until smooth. Refrigerate for at least 2 hours.

Serve with crackers or cucumber slices, or use a pastry bag to pipe mousse into puff pastry shells.   Makes 8 appetizers.

Serve with a Fumé Blanc or Chardonnay.

Easy Crab Appetizer

8 ounces cream cheese
2 tablespoons Chardonnay wine
8 ounces crab meat
2 tablespoons chopped green onions

½ teaspoon cream horseradish
¼ teaspoon seasoning salt
Dash of pepper
¼ cup chopped pistachios

Soften cream cheese with wine. Mix together all ingredients except the pistachios. Put mixture into an oven-proof baking dish.

Sprinkle chopped pistachios on top and bake in a 375 degree oven for 15 minutes. Serve with sliced fresh French bread baguettes or crackers.   Serves 6 as an appetizer.

Serve with a Chardonnay, Champagne (Brut) or Chenin Blanc.

Chicken Curry Salad

½ cup water
½ cup white wine
½ teaspoon dried thyme
½ teaspoon diced onion
½ teaspoon salt
2 chicken breasts, skinned
  and boned
½ cup mayonnaise
¼ cup orange juice

1 teaspoon curry powder
1 can water chestnuts, drained
  and coarsely chopped
½ can sliced palm hearts,
  drained
¾ cup coarsely chopped
  sugar-roasted peanuts
1 small can fried onion rings
1 cup fried chow mein noodles

Bring water, wine, thyme, onion and salt to a boil. Add chicken breasts, cover pan and simmer for 30 minutes. Remove from heat, and let breasts cool in the broth. (To microwave, bring broth to a boil, add chicken breasts and cover. Cook for 10 to 12 minutes on medium-low, and let cool in the broth.)

Cut chicken breasts into bite-size pieces. In a large bowl, mix mayonnaise, orange juice and curry powder thoroughly.

To the mayonnaise mixture, add in the chicken, water chestnuts, palm hearts and peanuts. Mix until everything is coated with the mayonnaise. Just before serving, stir in onion rings and noodles.

Serves 6.

Serve with a Chardonnay.

Fresh Broccoli and Crab Salad

4 fresh broccoli stems, finely shredded

1 cup of 1-inch asparagus pieces, steamed until crisp tender

1 medium cucumber, peeled and cut into thin strips 1 inch long

½ cup sliced green onions

1 red bell pepper, seeded and sliced fine

1 medium head butter lettuce, washed and broken into bite-size pieces

3 tablespoons fresh chopped dill

2 tablespoons fresh minced parsley

Juice of ½ lemon

Salt and pepper

Dressing (recipe follows)

1 cup crab meat, cleaned and chopped

1 hard-boiled egg, chopped

½ cup pinenuts

Combine broccoli, asparagus, cucumber, onion, red pepper, lettuce, dill and parsley. Mix well with lemon juice and salt and pepper. Prepare dressing.

DRESSING:
½ cup olive oil
½ cup mayonnaise

¼ cup Reisling wine

Mix all dressing ingredients thoroughly.

Pour dressing over tossed salad and mix well. Divide greens on 4 serving plates. Divide crab and place on top of greens with chopped egg and pinenuts sprinkled on top.   Serves 4.

Serve with a chilled Reisling.

Soups

COOKING WITH WINE

Thai Coconut Milk and Dungeness Crab Soup
with Curry Oil

1 cup Chardonnay wine
2 cans (12 ounces each)
  unsweetened coconut milk*
1 garlic clove, sliced
1 tablespoon sliced ginger
2 reeds of lemon grass,
  minced (reserve 3-inch long
  green tips for garnish)
2 limes (cut in half)
2 tablespoons minced cilantro
  stems

¼ cup Thai fish sauce*
1 serrano chile, seeded and
  minced
½ spaghetti squash
8 ounces crab meat
2 tablespoons butter
Curry Oil (recipe follows)
Lemon grass and cilantro
  sprigs for garnish

Reduce the wine to 1 tablespoon and set aside.

For the soup, combine the coconut milk, garlic, ginger, lemon grass, limes, cilantro, fish sauce, and the chile. Simmer 1 hour and strain. Add the wine reduction.

Steam the spaghetti squash for 30 to 45 minutes until the flesh can be separated with a fork.

CURRY OIL:
Dissolve 2 tablespoons curry powder in 3 tablespoons water. Then stir in 1 cup salad oil. Stir every hour for 4 hours and let sit overnight. Strain off oil from curry powder.

For presentation, heat the crab meat in 2 tablespoons water and 2 tablespoons butter. Heat the spaghetti squash in a little water and butter. Place the soup in a bowl, place a mound of spaghetti squash in the center and top with the crab meat. Drizzle the crab and soup with the Curry Oil and garnish with the green tips of lemon grass or cilantro sprigs. Serves 4 to 6.

*Available in the Oriental specialty food sections of most supermarkets.

Serve with a Chardonnay.

Zinfandel Holiday Soup

1 tablespoon olive oil
1 ½ pounds bulk sausage
1 cup chopped onion
3 cloves garlic, minced
2 pounds carrots, diced
2 cups diced celery
1 jar (26 ounces) spaghetti
  sauce

6 cans (10 ½ ounces each)
  beef broth
1 cup red Zinfandel wine
1 tablespoon dry chicken
  bouillon
2 teaspoons sugar
1 cup uncooked rice

In the olive oil, sauté sausage, onion and garlic in a large soup pot. After sausage is fully cooked, drain the fat. Then add remaining ingredients. Bring to a low boil. Cover and cook for 30 to 40 minutes on low until vegetables are done.

This recipe makes a big pot of soup that is great around the holidays. Serve with crusty French bread.   Serves 10 to 12.

Serve with a red Zinfandel or a Cabernet Sauvignon.

Onion Soup Au Vin

The flavor of this soup will be enhanced if the onions are cooked slowly.

4 tablespoons butter
6 medium onions, peeled and
  finely sliced
½ teaspoon salt
¼ teaspoon pepper

1 tablespoon flour
2 cups Chardonnay wine
7 cups chicken broth or stock
¼ cup freshly grated
  Parmesan cheese

Melt the butter in a soup pot. Add the onions. Stir, cover and simmer for 20 minutes, stirring occasionally. Add salt, pepper, flour and wine. Bring to a boil, stirring. Add the broth and simmer, uncovered, for 40 minutes. Serve sprinkled with Parmesan cheese. Serves 6.

Delicious with a Chardonnay or Chenin Blanc.

Smoked Tomato Soup

12 vine-ripened tomatoes
½ cup plus 4 tablespoons extra
  virgin olive oil
2 cups diced leeks (white and
  light green part)
1 cup chopped yellow onion
1 cup of a light Pinot Noir wine
⅛ cup diced smoked bacon

¼ cup minced garlic
2 tablespoon sea salt
1 tablespoon red wine vinegar
¼ teaspoon ground cayenne
  pepper
⅓ cup roughly chopped fresh
  parsley
Croutons (recipe follows)

Begin by preparing the tomatoes. Place whole tomatoes in a large bowl, sprinkle with 4 tablespoons of the olive oil, season with salt and black pepper. Cook in your barbecue or smoker for 20 minutes, or until tomatoes start to crack their skin. Don't forget to place a few wet wood chips (hickory or alder) on your coals so that the tomatoes pick up a nice smoky flavor. Set tomatoes aside to cool, then peel skins off.

To prepare the soup, place the ¼ cup of olive oil, leeks and onions in a soup pot. Cook over medium-high heat for about 10 minutes or until a light golden color appears.

Crush or roughly chop the smoked tomatoes. Add the tomatoes, wine, bacon, garlic, salt, vinegar and cayenne pepper to the soup pot. Cook over medium heat for 15 minutes. Add parsley. Incorporate the remaining ¼ cup olive oil. Divide into 6 preheated soup bowls, float 2 croutons on top and enjoy!   Serves 6.

CROUTONS:
Brush 12 pieces of thinly sliced French bread baguette with olive oil and toast in a 450 degree oven until golden brown. Rub with a garlic clove after cooling.

Serve with a Pinot Noir.

Hearty Lentil Soup

3 tablespoons olive oil
2 large onions, chopped
1 carrot, chopped
½ teaspoon dried marjoram
½ teaspoon dried thyme
3 cups beef stock
1 cup dry lentils, washed
1 can (14 ½ ounces) ready cut
  tomatoes, undrained

¼ cup chopped fresh parsley
½ cup Cabernet Sauvignon
  wine
Salt and pepper
⅔ cup grated Monterey jack
  cheese
2 to 3 strips bacon, cooked
  crisp and crumbled

Heat the olive oil in a large saucepan and sauté the onions and carrot for 3 to 5 minutes. Add the herbs and sauté for 1 minute more. Add the stock, lentils, tomatoes with their juice and the parsley.

Cover the saucepan and cook until the lentils are tender, 45 to 60 minutes. Add the wine. Taste for seasoning, adding salt and pepper if necessary.

To serve, place 2 tablespoons grated cheese in each serving bowl, pour in soup and top with crumbled bacon. This dish is especially delicious when served with hot corn muffins. May be made ahead and reheated -- it gets better.   Serves 4 to 6.

Serve with a Cabernet Sauvignon or Merlot.

Minestrone al Pesto

6 tomatoes, quartered and
  drizzled with olive oil
¼ pound pancetta or bacon,
  chopped
1 small onion, chopped
1 medium leek, sliced thin
2 stalks celery with leaves,
  finely chopped
1 carrot, finely chopped
½ medium green cabbage,
  chopped
½ cup water

½ cup white wine
1 cup fresh fava beans, or
  cooked red or white beans
6 cups chicken stock
¼ pound fresh green beans,
  cut into 1-inch pieces
¼ cup pesto
Salt and pepper
8 toasted 1-inch thick French
  bread slices, spread with
  additional ¼ cup pesto

Roast the tomatoes in a 425 degree oven for 20 to 30 minutes.
Reserve.

Place the pancetta in a large soup pot and sauté over medium-high
heat. Add the onion, leek, celery, carrot and cabbage to the pot and
cook 15 to 20 minutes to bring out the flavors in the vegetables.

Add the water, wine and fava beans and simmer over medium heat
for 15 minutes more.

Add the chicken stock; bring to a boil. Add the prepared tomatoes
and green beans; cook 10 minutes more. Add the pesto and season
with salt and pepper to taste. Place toasted pesto bread in soup
plates, surround with soup and serve.   Serves 8.

Serve with a white Zinfandel.

Pea Soup with Wine

½ pound bacon, finely
  chopped
2 large onions, chopped
3 large carrots, thinly sliced
2 large potatoes, diced
1 cup green split peas,
  uncooked
4 cups water

2 cups Chardonnay wine
1 ham hock
1 bay leaf
½ teaspoon black pepper,
  coarsely ground
Salt
2 tablespoons Sherry
Croutons

In a large kettle, sauté bacon until cooked, but not crisp. Set bacon aside. Add onions and sauté until limp. Add the carrots, potatoes, peas, water, wine, ham hock, bay leaf and pepper. Cover and simmer for 2 hours, stirring often.

Remove ham hock and set aside. Remove bay leaf and discard. Put soup through a sieve, or process in a blender until smooth. Cut the lean ham from the ham hock into small pieces. Return bacon and ham pieces to soup mixture.

Reheat and adjust seasonings; add Sherry. Float croutons on top of each serving.   Serves 6 to 8.

Serve with a Chardonnay.

Maritata, The Italian Marriage Soup

¼ pound unsalted butter
1 cup freshly grated asiago or
  Parmesan cheese
3 egg yolks
1 cup heavy cream
1 cup Chardonnay wine
4 cups chicken stock

¼ pound angel hair or fideo
  pasta
Salt and freshly ground
  pepper
Chopped parsley or chives for
  garnish

Cream butter in a food processor. Add grated cheese and process for 2 minutes. Add egg yolks, 1 at a time, processing briefly after each addition.

With processor running, slowly add cream through feed-tube. Scrape sides of bowl and process again.

Meanwhile, bring wine and chicken stock to a boil in a soup pot. Break pasta into pieces and drop into pot. Cook 8 minutes, or until pasta is al dente. Add some of the hot stock to the mixture in the food processor and process. Pour contents of processor into soup pot, bring to a simmer and season with salt and pepper to taste. Serve immediately, garnished with the parsley or chives.

Serves 4 to 6.

Serve with a Chardonnay.

Two-Pea Pea Soup

16 ounces dried split peas,
 cleaned and sorted
7 cups water
½ pound sliced ham
4 carrots, finely chopped
1 large or 2 medium onions,
 chopped

½ teaspoon dried or fresh
 thyme, crumbled
2 teaspoons sage
Salt and pepper
1 cup frozen peas
1 cup dry white wine
½ cup cream or half-and-half

Place the split peas and water in a soup pot. Add the ham, carrots, onions, thyme, sage, and salt and pepper. Cover and cook over low heat until peas are tender, stirring now and then. This will take an hour or more.

Remove the ham and cut into small pieces. Return ham pieces to soup. At this time, add the frozen peas. Reheat the soup just to a boil and until frozen peas are heated. Then add the wine and stir until reheated.

Just before serving, stir in the cream. Adjust seasonings if necessary. Serve with warm toasted croutons.   Serves 6 to 8.

Serve with a Sémillon or a Reisling.

Vegetable Bean Soup with Pistou

Pistou is the French version of Pesto.

1 tablespoon butter
1 tablespoon oil
1 medium onion, chopped
2 large leeks, washed and
  chopped
2 large carrots, chopped
2 large potatoes, peeled and
  diced
8 to 10 cups chicken stock
1 teaspoon salt, if desired
Pistou (recipe follows)
1 cup Chardonnay wine

¼ pound Swiss chard, chopped
½ pound green beans, cut into
  1-inch pieces
2 medium tomatoes, peeled
  and coarsely chopped
2 zucchini, halved lengthwise
  and sliced thin
2 cups cooked small dried
  beans (cannellini or small
  white beans)
1 cup small soup macaroni
Freshly ground black pepper

In a large stock pot, heat the butter and oil; add the onion, leeks and carrots. Sauté the vegetables for 5 minutes; add the potatoes, chicken stock and salt. Bring the soup to a boil, reduce the heat and simmer, uncovered, for 30 minutes. Meanwhile, prepare Pistou.

PISTOU:
3 cloves garlic
½ to 1 cup basil leaves

¼ cup olive oil
⅓ cup grated Parmesan cheese

In a food processor, process the garlic and basil, gradually adding the oil. Transfer the mixture to a bowl, and stir in the cheese. Set Pistou aside.

To the soup pot, add wine, Swiss chard, green beans, tomatoes, zucchini, cooked beans and pasta. Bring to a boil. Reduce the heat and simmer until the pasta is cooked, about 8 to 10 minutes. Stir in half the Pistou saving the rest to serve at the table. Season the soup with pepper and additional salt if desired.

Serves 10 to 12.

Enjoy with a Chardonnay.

Chicken Waterzooi

A classic Belgian dish that may be made with chicken or fish.

2 tablespoons butter
¼ cup olive oil
2 teaspoons nutmeg
1 teaspoons powdered thyme
2 leeks, chopped
1 celery top, chopped
2 carrots, chopped
2 onions, chopped
½ cup chopped fresh parsley

1 roasting chicken
2 cups white wine
4 cups chicken stock
1 bay leaf
2 egg yolks, slightly beaten
1 cup yogurt
Juice of 1 lemon
Salt and pepper

In a heavy pot, melt the butter and the olive oil together. Add the nutmeg and thyme; cook for 1 minute. Add the leeks, celery, carrots, onions, and parsley, and sauté for 1 to 2 minutes. Place the whole chicken on the vegetables, and add wine and stock to almost cover. Add the bay leaf, bring to a boil, and simmer covered for 45 minutes to an hour, until the chicken comes apart easily. Remove the chicken to a baking sheet to cool. Remove bay leaf and discard.

For a velvety texture, put the stock and vegetable mixture through a sieve, into a cooking pot; discard the contents of the sieve. (If you prefer a more chunky soup, you may leave out this step.) Keep warm over very low heat.

When the chicken is cool enough, discard the skin and remove the meat, pulling it away in good-sized pieces, if possible.

Add the egg yolks, ¾ cup of the yogurt, lemon juice, and salt and pepper to the vegetable mixture. Simmer for a few minutes to cook the egg yolks. Place the chicken in the pot and simmer to warm through. Serve in large soup plates topped with a dollop of yogurt.
Serves 6.

Serve with a Chardonnay or Reisling.

Spring Vegetable Chowder with Ham

3 strips uncooked bacon, chopped
2 tablespoons olive oil
2 medium brown onions, sliced
3 cloves garlic, minced
3 stalks celery, sliced ¼-inch thick
2 large potatoes, peeled and cubed
6 cups chicken stock
3 carrots, sliced ¼-inch thick
½ pound green beans, trimmed and cut into thirds

2 cups broccoli florets
2 medium tomatoes, seeded and cut into chunks
1 ½ cups halved mushrooms
1 can (14 ½ ounces) corn
1 teaspoon salt
½ teaspoon pepper
2 teaspoons cumin
Dash cayenne pepper
1 ¼ pounds ham, cubed
1 cup Chardonnay wine

In a large stock pot, cook bacon until brown. Remove bacon pieces; set aside.

To stock pot, add olive oil. Sauté onions, garlic and celery until tender, stirring approximately 5 minutes. Add potatoes, stir and cook for 10 minutes. Add chicken stock.

Transfer half the mixture to a food processor and purée until smooth. Return to stock pot. Add remaining vegetables and season with spices. Bring to a slow boil. Reduce heat to low. Simmer, uncovered, for approximately 40 minutes or until vegetables are tender. Add ham, bacon bits and wine.   Serves 6 to 8.

Serve with a Chardonnay or Pinot Blanc.

Leek Soup

2 tablespoons butter
1 large onion, finely chopped
2 bunches leeks, thoroughly
  cleaned and sliced
6 cups chicken stock
2 cups dry white wine
2 teaspoons chopped fresh
  tarragon (or ½ teaspoon
  dried)

3 medium potatoes, diced
Salt and freshly ground black
  pepper
1 cup cream
¼ cup finely chopped fresh
  parsley
½ cup grated Gruyère or
  fontina cheese

In a large saucepan, melt the butter. Sauté onion and leeks until soft. Add stock, wine tarragon, potatoes, salt and pepper. Cover and simmer for 15 minutes, or until tender. Purée in a food processor or mash with a potato masher.

Reheat and stir in cream and fresh parsley. Ladle into bowls. Sprinkle grated cheese on each serving.   Serves 8.

Serve with a Cabernet Sauvignon.

Carrot Chardonnay Soup

2 large onions, sliced
3 cloves garlic, minced
2 shallots, minced
4 tablespoons butter
10 to 15 carrots, peeled and
  chopped
4 cups Chardonnay wine
2 cups water
1 inch of fresh ginger, minced

2 sprigs fresh rosemary
Honey to taste
Salt and pepper
1 cup whipping cream

GARNISH:
½ cup whipping cream
¼ teaspoon nutmeg

Sauté onions, garlic and shallots in butter until limp and translucent. Add carrots and coat with butter. Let cook for just a few minutes. Add the wine and water. Add the minced ginger and rosemary. Simmer until carrots are very tender. Purée vegetables until smooth. Return to pan with cooking liquids.

Adjust seasoning with honey, salt and pepper. Add cream a little at a time. Reheat on low heat. It will round out and smooth the flavors.

To garnish, whip the ½ cup cream and set aside. Fold the nutmeg into the cream and mix well. Float dollops of cream on top of soup.
Serves 6.

Serve with a Chardonnay.

Butternut Ginger Bisque

1 butternut squash (about 4 cups of cooked purée)	½ cup flour
½ cup unsalted butter	6 cups chicken stock
1 cup diced onion	1 cup dry Chenin Blanc wine
2 teaspoons grated fresh ginger	1 cup whipping cream
	½ cup chopped fresh parsley
	Nutmeg

Peel the butternut squash and remove the seeds. Dice the squash into 1-inch squares. Steam squash until tender. Purée cooked squash and measure 4 cups of purée; set aside.

Melt the butter in a heavy saucepan over medium heat. Add onion and ginger; cook until onions are transparent, stirring occasionally. Add flour and cook about 3 minutes.

Gradually add stock while stirring. Bring to a boil. Add puréed butternut squash. Add wine, stir; then add the cream. Heat until almost boiling. Quickly stir in parsley.

Serve with a sprinkle of nutmeg floating in each bowl.   Serves 6.

Serve this soup with a Chenin Blanc.

Red Bell Pepper Soup

3 tablespoons butter
1 large white onion, peeled
  and chopped
6 large red bell peppers,
  seeded and coarsely
  chopped

1 clove garlic
 6 cups chicken stock
1 cup cream
Salt and pepper
½ cup Chardonnay wine
Sour cream (optional)

In a heavy saucepan, melt the butter over medium heat. Add the onion and cook, stirring occasionally, until the onion is soft and brown.

Add the bell peppers and stir until they are soft. Add the garlic clove and chicken stock, increase heat and bring to a boil. Let mixture cook until bell peppers are completely softened, about 30 minutes.

Remove from heat and purée in batches in a blender or food processor. Return soup purée mixture to a new pot, add the cream and bring to a boil. Reduce heat to a simmer and reduce for 10 minutes until slightly thickened. Season to taste with salt and pepper. Add the wine.

Serve hot, or let cool and refrigerate. Before serving, add a dab of sour cream to each hot bowl of soup.   Serves 4 to 6.

Serve with a Chardonnay.

Corn Chowder

1 large white onion, diced
2 carrots, peeled and diced
2 stalks celery, diced
3 strips bacon, diced
3 tablespoons corn oil
2 cloves garlic, minced
1 cup white wine
3 cups fresh corn cut from
  cobs (approximately 6 cobs)

3 cups chicken stock
1 cup cream
2 tablespoons chopped fresh
  thyme
2 tablespoons chopped fresh
  basil
Salt and pepper
2 drops Tabasco sauce

Sauté onions, carrots, celery and bacon in the oil until soft.

Over medium heat, add garlic and cook for approximately 1 minute. Add wine and cook 3 minutes. Add corn, chicken stock, cream and thyme. Cook until tender. Add basil, and salt and pepper to taste.

Remove ⅓ of the soup and purée in a food processor or blender. Return to remainder of soup. Add Tabasco sauce and stir. Serve with fresh toasted croutons.   Serves 6.

Serve with any dry white wine.

Tomato and Tarragon Soup

4 tablespoons butter or margarine
1 onion, chopped
1 stalk celery, thinly sliced
1 carrot, thinly sliced
5 tomatoes, roughly chopped
3 tablespoons tomato purée or paste
3 cups tomato juice

2 tablespoons chopped fresh tarragon
1 bay leaf
Salt and pepper
¼ cup Pinot Noir wine
2 tablespoons cornstarch
Pinch sugar
Chopped celery leaves for garnish

Melt the butter in a saucepan; cook the onion, celery and carrot slowly until soft. Add the tomatoes, tomato purée, tomato juice, tarragon, bay leaf and salt and pepper. Cover and simmer for 20 minutes. Remove the bay leaf. Purée the soup in a food processor or blender. Strain out the seeds and tomato skins through a fine sieve, and return soup to saucepan.

Mix the wine and cornstarch together and add some of the hot soup. Stir into the cooking soup until soup thickens. Add a pinch of sugar if necessary to bring out the tomato flavor. Serve garnished with the chopped celery leaves.   Serves 4.

Serve a Pinot Noir or Merlot with this.

Carrot and Basil Soup

3 tablespoons butter or
  margarine
2 medium onions, finely
  chopped
6 carrots, peeled and diced
2 large potatoes, peeled and
  diced
4 cups chicken or vegetable
  stock

2 cups water
2 tablespoon chopped basil
1 bay leaf
Pinch of nutmeg
Juice of ½ lemon
Salt and pepper
½ cup Chardonnay wine
½ cup cream
Fresh basil leaves, for garnish

Melt the butter in a heavy-bottomed pan; cook the onions over a low
heat to soften. Add the carrots and potatoes. Cook for 2 minutes,
stirring occasionally. Add the stock, water, basil, bay leaf, nutmeg
and lemon juice. Season to taste with salt and pepper. Cook for 20
to 25 minutes.

When vegetables are tender, remove the bay leaf and allow the
soup to cool slightly. Purée in a food processor or blender. Add
wine. Return to low heat, slowly stirring in cream. Garnish with
fresh basil leaves.   Serves 4 to 6.

Serve with a Chardonnay.

Black Bean Soup with 2 Salsas

1 ½ cups black beans, rinsed and sorted
1 small onion, diced into small squares
1 garlic clove, finely chopped
1 can (16 ounces) peeled tomatoes, with the juice reserved

½ chipotle chile, seeded and minced
½ bunch cilantro, chopped
½ cup Zinfandel wine
Roasted Red Pepper Salsa (recipe follows)
Cilantro-Pineapple Salsa (recipe follows)

Drain beans and put them in a soup pot with enough cold water to cover them by a couple of inches. Bring to a boil and skim off the foam that rises to the surface; then add the onions and garlic. Lower heat and cook until the onions are soft, about 15 minutes. Add the tomatoes and their juice, the chile, half the cilantro, and a dash of salt. Simmer until the beans are tender, about 1 hour. Occasionally give them a stir while they're cooking.

When done, taste for salt, stir in remaining cilantro and wine. Serve over polenta with Roasted Red Pepper Salsa and Cilantro-Pineapple Salsa.   Serves 6.

ROASTED RED PEPPER SALSA:
1 small garlic clove
4 large fire-roasted red bell peppers, seeded
½ cup non-fat sour cream
½ teaspoon lemon juice

2 tablespoons chopped fresh basil
¼ teaspoon ground pepper
1 teaspoon anchovy paste

Mince garlic in food processor. Add bell pepper, sour cream and remaining ingredients. Process until smooth.

CILANTRO-PINEAPPLE SALSA:
1 ½ cups coarsely chopped fresh pineapple

2 tablespoons minced fresh cilantro

Place chopped pineapple in food processor and pulse 5 times. Spoon into bowl and stir in cilantro.

Serve with a Zinfandel.

Sherry Shrimp Soup

1 ½ pounds shrimp
1 quart water
4 to 5 celery leaves
1 tablespoon salt
7 tablespoons butter

1 medium onion, chopped
8 tablespoons flour
2 cups chicken broth
1 cup cream
⅔ cup golden Sherry

Cook shrimp in 1 quart boiling water with celery leaves and salt. Boil 5 minutes. Drain shrimp and reserve liquid. Clean shrimp and chop fine; set aside.

In a stock pot, sauté onion in butter. When onions are soft, add the flour and blend well. Add the chicken broth. Stir until thick; then add reserved shrimp liquid. Simmer for 5 minutes, then add the shrimp and cream. Stir while heating. Add Sherry just before serving.

Serves 6.

Serve with any dry white wine.

Creamed Avocado Soup

This is one from my own family file and I use it frequently when avocados are in season. Try to get the large Haas type, if possible.

4 large ripe avocados
3 cups chicken broth
½ teaspoon salt

Pinch white pepper
1 cup light cream
3 tablespoons sherry

Peel, pit and cube the avocados, then purée them in a blender.

In a saucepan, mix avocado purée, chicken broth, salt and pepper. Heat to boiling point, stirring occasionally. Stir in light cream. Cover and simmer 10 minutes. Add sherry. Serve soup hot; garnish each bowl with croutons.

Serves 6.

Serve with a dry white wine.

Sherry Mushroom Soup

1 pound fresh mushrooms,
  sliced
1 large onion, thinly sliced
2 tablespoons butter or
  margarine
4 cups beef broth

¾ cup cream Sherry
2 tablespoons flour
6 slices French bread
½ cup shredded Gruyere
  cheese

In a 4-quart saucepan, cook mushrooms and onion in butter until onion is soft, stirring for 1 to 2 minutes. Add broth and simmer, covered, for 10 minutes. Mix ¼ cup of the Sherry and flour until flour is dissolved. Stir into soup. Cook for 5 minutes until soup thickens, then add remaining ½ cup Sherry, stirring well.

Preheat broiler. Place bread slices on a baking sheet and sprinkle with cheese. Broil until cheese is melted. Pour soup into 6 serving bowls. Float a slice of cheese toast in each bowl.   Serves 6.

Serve with a Reisling or Chenin Blanc.

Creamed Corn and Red Pepper Soup

1 onion, chopped
2 red bell peppers, chopped
  fine
3 tablespoons butter
4 cups fresh corn cut from cob
  (about 8 cobs)

4 cups chicken stock
1 cup heavy cream
¼ cup Dry Sherry
Salt and pepper
Cayenne pepper

Sauté onion and peppers in the butter for 10 minutes; do not brown. Add corn and sauté for 5 minutes. Add stock and simmer for 15 minutes. Purée; return to soup pot. Add cream and Sherry. Reheat soup. Season with salt and pepper to taste. Serve with a sprinkle of cayenne in each bowl.   Serves 4 to 6.

Serve with a Reisling or Chardonnay.

Hazelnut and Squash Soup

1 ½ cups mashed cooked
  summer squash
1 cup finely chopped
  hazelnuts
½ cup finely chopped onion
1 quart chicken broth or stock

Salt
¼ teaspoon pepper
2 tablespoons butter or
  margarine
¼ cup Sherry
Hazelnuts for garnish

Combine squash, hazelnuts, onion and broth in saucepan. Bring to a boil. Cover and simmer for 30 minutes, stirring occasionally. Stir in salt to taste, pepper, butter and Sherry.

Spread sliced hazelnuts in a shallow pan and toast in a 275 degree oven for approximately 20 minutes, stirring to prevent over-browning.

Serve garnished with sliced toasted hazelnuts.   Serves 6 to 8.

A Chardonnay or any dry white wine will go well with this.

Pastas & Grains

COOKING WITH WINE

Chicken Breasts with Lobster, Mushroom and Wine Sauce on Vermicelli

8 ounces vermicelli pasta
4 chicken breasts
6 tablespoons butter
¾ pound cooked lobster or
  crab meat, cut into cubes
2 large red bell peppers,
  sliced

1 cup sliced fresh mushrooms
2 tablespoons finely chopped
  fresh basil
Salt and pepper
1 cup Reisling wine
½ cup grated fresh mozzarella
  cheese

Prepare vermicelli in boiling, salted water according to package instructions. Drain. Set aside and keep warm.

Sauté the chicken breasts in 2 tablespoons of the butter for 5 to 6 minutes on each side or until cooked through. Set aside and keep warm.

In the same pan, sauté the lobster, bell peppers, mushrooms and the basil. Season with salt and pepper. Add ½ cup of the wine; heat. Then thicken with 2 tablespoons of the butter.

Place a chicken breast and a serving of vermicelli on each heated plate. Top which with lobster/pepper mixture.

Add the remaining ½ cup wine and remaining 2 tablespoons butter to the pan and deglaze. Cook rapidly to thicken and pour over chicken and pasta. Sprinkle with mozzarella cheese before serving.

Serves 4.

Serve with a Johannisberg Reisling.

Fettuccine with Red Pepper Sauce

3 tablespoons butter
2 large red bell peppers, cut
  into very thin strips
3 cloves garlic, minced
¾ teaspoon cayenne pepper
1 cup white wine

½ cup cream
¾ cup grated Parmesan
  cheese
12 ounces fettuccine pasta
Salt and pepper
½ cup minced fresh basil

Melt the butter in a large skillet over medium heat. Add bell peppers, garlic and cayenne; stir to blend. Cover skillet; cook until peppers are tender, stirring occasionally, about 7 minutes. Add the wine; stir to blend. Add cream and simmer until liquid is slightly thickened, about 5 minutes.

At this time, add ½ cup of the Parmesan cheese, stirring. Remove from heat while you prepare the fettuccine.

Cook fettuccine according to package instructions until just tender. Drain and add to pepper sauce. Toss fettuccine in sauce; season with salt and pepper, and fresh basil. Serve with the remaining ¼ cup Parmesan cheese sprinkled on top.   Serves 4.

Serve with a dry Zinfandel or Fumé Blanc.

Zesty Mushroom Marinara

2 tablespoons olive oil
1 small white onion, chopped
3 cloves garlic, minced
¼ pound mushrooms, sliced
½ cup Zinfandel wine
1 pound fresh or canned
  tomatoes (14 ½ ounces),
  diced

1 can (8 ounces) tomato
  sauce
¼ teaspoon fresh or dried
  oregano
¼ teaspoon crushed red
  pepper
Polenta (recipe follows)
Parsley for garnish

Heat oil over medium heat. Add onion and cook, stirring, for about 5 minutes. Add garlic and mushrooms. Cook uncovered until mushrooms are lightly browned. Add wine and simmer for about 3 minutes. Add tomatoes, tomato sauce, oregano and red pepper. Bring to a boil, reduce heat and simmer, uncovered, for about 10 minutes. Meanwhile, prepare Polenta.

POLENTA:
1 cup polenta
4 cups water
1 teaspoon salt

2 tablespoons butter
¼ cup grated Parmesan cheese

Gradually add polenta to boiling salted water, stirring constantly until thickened. Cook, stirring, for approximately 25 minutes. Blend in butter and Parmesan cheese. Pour into a 9 × 9-inch buttered pan or platter. Allow to set until firm, 1 hour. Cut in squares or triangles. Sauté in small amount of butter to heat before serving.

Place squares of polenta on serving plates and serve hot marinara sauce over polenta. Garnish with parsley.   Makes 8 servings.

Serve with a Zinfandel.

South of the Border Chicken Pasta

2 pounds boneless, skinless
  chicken breasts
1 package taco seasoning mix
1 tablespoon olive oil
8 ounces linguine or rotelli
  pasta

8 ounces mild salsa
3 tablespoons apricot jam
½ cup Riesling wine
1 cup whole pitted olives
Romano cheese, grated

Remove all fat from chicken and cut into ¾-inch cubes. Shake dry taco seasoning onto chicken and coat well. Sauté coated chicken pieces in olive oil until lightly browned; set aside.

Cook pasta according to package directions. Drain and set aside.

Combine salsa, jam and wine. Add to chicken in skillet and simmer for 10 minutes. Add olives and cook another 2 to 3 minutes. Serve over pasta, and sprinkle generously with grated Romano cheese.

Serves 4.

Serve with a Riesling.

Penne Pasta with Sun-Dried Tomatoes and Mushrooms

Zesty sun-dried tomatoes are complemented by the earthy flavors of shiitake mushrooms, garlic and the lush flavors of the wine.

1 package (11 ounces) penne pasta
2 tablespoons olive oil
1 medium yellow onion, sliced ¼-inch thick
1 tablespoon chopped garlic
1 package (½ ounce) dried shiitake mushrooms (reconstituted according to package directions and sliced in ¼-inch strips)
½ cup Chardonnay wine
1 package (3 ounces) sun-dried tomatoes (softened according to package directions and cut in half)
½ teaspoon crushed red pepper
Salt and pepper
2 tablespoons butter
2 tablespoons chopped fresh basil
1 cup basil jack cheese, grated

Cook pasta following package directions. In large non-stick frying pan, heat olive oil until it starts to smoke. Add the onion and sauté until golden brown (about 5 minutes). Add garlic and mushrooms and sauté 2 minutes longer. Add wine and tomatoes, reduce liquid until almost dry. Add crushed red pepper. Salt and pepper to taste. Remove from heat and stir in butter.

Toss mixture thoroughly with pasta and basil. Top with grated cheese. Goes great with a Caesar salad and garlic bread.

Serves 6 as a first course; 4 as an entrée.

Serve with a Chardonnay.

Fettuccine with Caramelized Onions

1 cube butter (or ½ cube butter
    and ¼ cup olive oil)
8 yellow onions, sliced thin

1 pound fettuccine
¼ cup Pinot Noir wine
Salt and pepper

Melt butter in a large skillet. Mound sliced onions high in the pan; they will cook down considerably. Cook over medium-high heat, with minimal stirring, for 1 hour or until the onions are a deep caramel color.

Cook the fettuccine until tender. Drain, rinse, and place in a warm serving bowl.

Add the wine to the onion mixture and cook over medium-high heat for a few minutes to deglaze the pan. Add the onion mixture to the warm pasta and toss to combine. Season with salt and pepper to taste.   Serves 4 to 6.

Serve with a Pinot Noir or your favorite white wine.

Zucchini Lasagna

1 pound lasagna noodles
8 medium zucchini, cleaned
  and sliced lengthwise
2 tablespoons olive oil
2 cans artichoke hearts,
  drained and chopped
2 cloves garlic, minced
1 yellow onion, chopped

2 medium tomatoes, chopped
½ cup dry white wine
2 to 3 tablespoons chopped
  fresh basil leaves
2 cups good white sauce
Parmesan cheese (optional)

Bring a large pot of water to a boil. Add the lasagna noodles and cook until tender. Drain, rinse and set aside.

Sauté the zucchini slices in 1 tablespoon of the olive oil in a non-stick pan until lightly browned. Remove from pan and set aside.

Add artichoke hearts, garlic, onion, tomatoes and the remaining olive oil to pan. Sauté a few minutes until flavors begin to blend. Add wine and 1 tablespoon of the basil to the mixture. Cook for a few minutes, then set aside.

Warm the white sauce. Add a dash of nutmeg; salt and pepper to taste.

Place ⅓ of the zucchini slices in the bottom of a baking pan. Cover with a thin layer of vegetable mixture, then a layer of noodles and one of white sauce, sprinkling occasionally with chopped basil. Continue layering until all ingredients are used. The final layer should be white sauce with a sprinkling of the remaining basil leaves.

Cover with foil and bake for 30 minutes in a 400 degree oven. Remove the foil for the last 10 minutes to brown the sauce.

Serves 8.

Serve with a Barbera.

Pasta Rustica, an Italian Fisherman Classic

¼ cup olive oil
2 cloves garlic, minced
6 plum tomatoes, quartered
  and cut into ½-inch slices
3 tablespoons finely chopped
  fresh parsley
⅓ cup finely chopped fresh
  basil
1 tablespoon grated lemon
  rind
½ cup Sauvignon Blanc wine

¾ pound lemon or gray sole,
  cut into ½-inch strips
15 kalamata olives, pitted and
  cut in half
1 teaspoon salt
Freshly ground black pepper
½ pound penne rigate (or
  other tubular pasta), cooked
2 tablespoons finely chopped
  fresh parsley for garnish

In a wok or large skillet, heat olive oil. Add garlic and cook over medium heat for 2 minutes. Do not brown.

Add tomatoes, parsley, basil, lemon rind and wine. Cook 3 minutes over high heat. Add fish, olives, salt and pepper. Cook 2 minutes until fish is just cooked. Add cooked pasta and toss thoroughly with sauce.

Serve in 4 flat soup plates. Garnish with chopped parsley.

Makes 4 servings.

Serve with a Sauvignon Blanc.

Pasta Stuffed Peppers

Peppers never tasted this good -- substantial enough for a meal or great to do ahead for a barbecue.

2 large, ripe tomatoes
¼ cup red wine
2 strips pancetta or lean bacon
2 small yellow onions, peeled
  and chopped
2 cloves garlic, crushed
Grated rind of 1 lemon

4 leaves chard, chopped
¼ pound orzo or seed pasta
Olive oil
Salt and pepper
4 large green, yellow or red
  bell peppers

Place the whole tomatoes on a flat pan in a 400 degree oven for one hour. Deglaze the pan with the wine, reserving wine. Chop the tomatoes, reserving the juice, then set aside.

Coarsely chop the pancetta and sauté until crisp; remove to a paper towel. Sauté the onions, garlic and lemon rind in the same pan. Cook over medium-low heat until the onions are translucent. Add the chard and sauté 5 minutes, scraping the pan to get all the flavorful juices. Add the tomatoes, their juice and the pancetta to this mixture.

Bring a large pot of water to a rolling boil. Add the pasta and cook until done. Drain and reserve.

Place the pasta and the pancetta/tomato mixture into a large bowl. Add a little olive oil, if necessary. Salt and pepper to taste. Toss to combine.

Slice off the tops of the peppers; reserve tops. (The tops will be the "lids" once the peppers are stuffed.) Remove the seeds. Fit the peppers snugly into a casserole dish. Spoon the stuffing mixture into the peppers, and replace the lids. Drizzle with olive oil and sprinkle with salt and pepper. Bake in a 375 degree oven for 45 minutes.   Serves 4.

Serve with a Barbera or Chianti.

Smoked Salmon & Cucumber Linguine

3 tablespoons olive oil
½ cup finely chopped scallions
  (white and green parts)
½ cup Chardonnay wine
1 cup heavy cream
3 tablespoons butter
¼ cup grated Parmesan
  cheese
⅔ cup frozen peas, defrosted

⅔ cup peeled, seeded and
  diced cucumber
½ pound smoked salmon, cut
  into ⅛-inch strips
8 cherry tomatoes, cut in half
¾ pound linguine, cooked
2 tablespoons finely chopped
  parsley

Heat olive oil and scallions in non-stick skillet for 1 minute. Add wine, cream, butter and half of the Parmesan cheese. Cook over high heat for 2 minutes until sauce begins to thicken.

Add peas, diced cucumber, smoked salmon and tomatoes. Cook over high heat for 1 minute. Add linguine to pan and mix well with sauce.

Divide pasta evenly into bowls. Sprinkle with chopped parsley and remaining Parmesan cheese.   Makes 4 servings.

Serve with a Chardonnay or Fumé Blanc.

Super Scallops Pasta Supper

¾ pound pasta (bowties, fusilli, or other thick shape)
2 tablespoons olive oil
1 medium red onion, sliced fine
3 medium zucchini, sliced ⅓-inch thick
6 green onions, sliced (equal parts of white and green)
2 cups quartered fresh mushrooms
1 teaspoon minced fresh garlic
⅓ cup Fumé Blanc wine
⅓ cup minced fresh basil

1 teaspoon minced lemon zest
1 teaspoon minced lime zest
2 tablespoons lemon juice
⅓ cup bottled clam juice
1 tablespoon tomato paste
¼ teaspoon ground white pepper
1 ¼ pounds sea scallops, cut into ⅓-inch slices
⅓ cup half-and-half
½ cup grated Parmesan cheese
2 tablespoons minced fresh parsley, for garnish

The on-stove cooking time of this great dish is not that long, so it is best to have all the "slicing and dicing" prepared and ready. Preheating the individual serving dishes for any pasta is a must. Put them in a 250 degree oven 30 minutes before serving.

Cook pasta according to package directions -- do not overcook! Drain and set aside.

In a large saucepan over medium-high heat in the olive oil, sauté the onion, zucchini, green onions and mushrooms for 5 minutes. Add garlic and cook for 2 minutes more. Add the wine, basil, citrus zests, lemon juice, clam juice, tomato paste, white pepper, and salt to taste. Simmer a few minutes; add scallops, cook 3 minutes. Then add the half-and-half.

Add pasta to the saucepan. Toss to combine. Add cheese to blend. Serve on heated serving dishes. Garnish with minced parsley.
Serves 4 to 6.

Serve with a seasonal salad, French bread, and a Fumé Blanc.

Green Pasta with Herbs

1 pound fusilli noodles	1 tablespoon red chili powder
2 tablespoons butter	⅓ cup finely chopped basil
2 tablespoons olive oil	⅓ cup finely chopped mint
4 cloves garlic, crushed	⅓ cup finely chopped parsley
1 cup dry white wine	Salt
3 twists of a black pepper grinder	Romano cheese, grated

Cook the noodles until tender; keep warm.

Melt the butter and olive oil in a large skillet. Add the garlic and cook over low heat until it begins to brown slightly. Add the wine and cook until liquid is reduced by half. Add the spices and herbs. Toss with the pasta. Salt to taste. Sprinkle with Romano cheese.

Serves 4.

Serve with a Sauvignon Blanc.

Saffron Pilaf

1 tablespoon butter	1 cinnamon stick (2 inches)
1 cup long grain rice	¼ teaspoon crumbled saffron threads
½ cup dry white wine	
1 ½ cups unsalted chicken stock	½ teaspoon salt
	¼ teaspoon freshly ground black pepper
1 teaspoon whole coriander seeds, crushed	¼ teaspoon paprika

Heat the butter until bubbly in a heavy saucepan. Sauté the rice for 2 to 3 minutes, stirring constantly with a wooden spoon to coat the grains well.

Add remaining ingredients and mix well. Bring to a boil, cover, and reduce heat as low as possible. Simmer for 20 minutes. Turn off heat and let rest, covered, for 5 minutes before serving. Serves 4.

This subtle pilaf goes well with grilled meats and a Pinot Noir.

Penne Pasta In Creamy Tomato Sausage Sauce

1 tablespoon butter
1 tablespoon olive oil
1 large onion, thinly sliced
3 garlic cloves, minced
1 pound Italian sausages
1 cup dry white wine
1 can (14 ½ ounces) diced
  peeled tomatoes, with juice

1 cup cream
6 tablespoons chopped Italian
  parsley
1 pound penne pasta
Salt and pepper
1 cup freshly grated Parmesan
  cheese

Melt butter and oil in a heavy skillet over medium high heat. Add onion and garlic. Sauté until golden brown and tender, about 7 minutes.

Remove sausages from casings and break up into small pieces. Add to skillet and cook until browned, about 10 minutes. Add the wine and tomatoes. Bring to a boil for 2 to 3 minutes. Add cream and simmer until sauce thickens, about 5 minutes. Stir in 4 tablespoons of the parsley. Cover and remove from heat.

Cook pasta according to package directions. Return sauce to a simmer. Season to taste with salt and pepper. Pour sauce over pasta. Add ½ cup of the Parmesan cheese and toss to coat. Serve on warm plates and sprinkle with remaining cheese and parsley.

Serves 6.

Serve with a Barbera or Merlot.

Vin Zin Pasta Sauce with Sausage

¼ cup olive oil
6 Italian sausages
6 large cloves garlic, peeled
  and chopped
1 medium onion, peeled and
  chopped
2 cans (8 ounces each)
  tomatoes, undrained
1 can (5 ½ ounces) tomato
  paste

2 teaspoons dried oregano
2 teaspoons dried basil
1 cinnamon stick (6 inches)
  broken in half
¼ teaspoon hot red pepper
  flakes
Salt and freshly ground black
  pepper
½ cup Zinfandel wine

Heat oil in large saucepan. Add sausages and fry until browned, about 10 minutes. Drain and set aside.

In the same pan add garlic and onion. Cook until onion is tender, about 4 minutes. Add remaining ingredients. Lower heat and simmer for about 30 minutes. Add sausage and simmer for another 1 to 3 hours, stirring occasionally.

Serve over hot pasta. Pass grated Parmesan cheese to garnish. This sauce is best served over a heavier pasta such as penne, mostaccioli or rigatoni.   Serves 6.

Serve with a Zinfandel.

Fettuccine with Spring Vegetables and Prawns

4 tablespoons light olive oil
2 cloves garlic, minced
4 green onions, thinly sliced
½ pound mushrooms, wiped
  clean and thinly sliced
¼ cup diced red bell pepper
¼ cup thinly sliced yellow
  crookneck squash
1 pound medium shrimp,
  peeled and deveined
½ cup Chardonnay wine
1 teaspoon crushed red
  pepper
1 cup asparagus tips, cut into
  1-inch pieces
1 pound fresh fettuccine pasta
4 tablespoons light cream
3 tablespoons chopped fresh
  parsley, thyme, and oregano
Freshly grated Parmesan
  cheese

Begin to heat 3 to 4 quarts of salted water for cooking the fettuccine.

Heat olive oil in sauté pan over medium heat. Add the garlic, onions, mushrooms, bell pepper and squash. Sauté until just barely softened. Remove from pan and keep warm. Add shrimp to sauté pan and shake to coat with remaining oil in pan. Pour in wine, add crushed red pepper and cook until shrimp begins to turn pink. Add asparagus and simmer over low heat for 4 to 5 minutes.

In the meantime, cook fettuccine in boiling water until al dente -- it should be tender, but slightly firm. Return reserved vegetables to the sauté pan, stir in cream and immediately remove from heat. Season with salt and pepper. Toss with fettuccine. Sprinkle with fresh herbs and Parmesan cheese, and serve.   Serves 4

Accompany with crusty French bread and a glass of Chardonnay!

Creamed Mushroom Mostaccioli

1 pound mushrooms	1 cup Dry Vermouth
1 tablespoon butter	½ cup cream
1 tablespoon olive oil	¼ teaspoon nutmeg
½ cup minced onion	8 ounces mostaccioli* pasta
Salt and pepper	¼ cup crumbled blue cheese

Wash, remove stems and slice the mushrooms. Melt the butter and olive oil in a skillet. Sauté the onion until soft; add the mushrooms. Season with salt and pepper to taste, and continue cooking over medium heat until mushrooms are just golden brown, about 5 minutes. Add Vermouth; blend well. Add cream and nutmeg and continue to stir until sauce thickens. Set aside and keep warm.

Cook pasta according to package directions; drain. Pour warm sauce over pasta, gently tossing to distribute sauce. Serve with a sprinkle of crumbled blue cheese on top.   Serves 6.

*A large, tube pasta.

Serve with a Chardonnay.

Lemon Basil Risotto Cakes

2 cups chicken stock
3 tablespoons olive oil
1 shallot, minced
Zest of ½ a lemon
1 cup arborio rice

1 cup Chardonnay wine
3 to 4 tablespoons grated
  Parmesan cheese
Salt and pepper
2 tablespoons chopped basil

Bring the stock to a simmer in a saucepan.

Heat 1 tablespoon of the olive oil in a heavy-bottomed pan over medium heat and add the minced shallot. Stir while cooking, 2 to 3 minutes, to soften. Add lemon zest and rice, stirring for about a minute to coat with oil.

Add the hot stock 1 cup at a time, allowing each cup to be absorbed before you add the next. Stir the rice continuously. When all the stock has been absorbed, add the wine and stir while it is absorbed. The rice should develop a creamy, almost porridge-like consistency, but the grains should still have a bit of a bite. If the rice is too tough, add some more wine and let it cook into the rice until soft. Total cooking time is about 20 to 25 minutes.

Take the pan off the heat. Stir in the cheese, salt, pepper, and basil. Be careful adding the salt, because the cheese is salty. Cover and allow the risotto to cool completely in the refrigerator. Form the cool risotto into patties, 2 to 5 inches wide and about ¼-inch thick. Set aside.

Heat oven to 200 degrees. Heat the remaining 2 tablespoons olive oil over medium heat in a heavy-bottomed frying pan. Add the patties in batches, browning each side for a few minutes. Keep the browned risotto cakes in the warm oven while you finish browning the rest. Serve immediately.   Serves 4 to 6.

Enjoy with a Chardonnay or a Sauvignon Blanc.

Noodles with Lemon Caper Sauce

8 ounces egg noodles
3 tablespoons butter
1 tablespoon olive oil
1 clove garlic, minced
½ cup dry white wine
2 tablespoons capers
1 tablespoon lemon juice
1 teaspoon lemon zest

2 tablespoons chopped fresh
 basil
Salt and pepper
2 tablespoons chopped fresh
 parsley
¼ cup grated Parmesan
 cheese

Cook the noodles according to package directions; drain. Add 1 tablespoon of the butter and toss. Set aside, keeping pasta warm.

Cook garlic in remaining butter and the olive oil. Stir in wine, capers, lemon juice, lemon zest, basil, and salt and pepper to taste. Heat until hot. Toss with noodles. Sprinkle with fresh parsley and Parmesan cheese.   Serves 6.

Serve with a Chardonnay, Sémillon or Reisling.

Poppy Seed Noodles

These noodles are very good served with chicken or beef.

8 ounces wide egg noodles
3 tablespoons butter
1 cup thinly sliced green
 onions

2 teaspoons poppy seeds
½ cup white wine
Salt and pepper

Cook noodles in a medium saucepan of boiling, salted water until just tender, but still firm to the bite; drain well. Set aside, covered, to keep warm. In the same saucepan, melt the butter; add green onions, poppy seeds, noodles and wine. Toss and stir gently to coat the noodles. Add more wine if noodles are dry. Season with salt and pepper.   Serves 4.

Serve with Sauvignon Blanc or Reisling.

Shiitake Mushroom Risotto

2 tablespoons extra virgin olive
  oil
1 onion, chopped
½ pound fresh shiitake
  mushrooms, chopped
¼ cup milk
¼ cup grated Parmesan
  cheese
1 pound arborio rice

3 cups dry white wine
5 cups homemade vegetable
  stock (or 5 vegetable bouillon
  cubes in 5 cups water)
2 cups asparagus pieces,
  blanched and dried
¼ cup chopped sun-dried
  tomatoes
Pinch of saffron

Heat the olive oil in a large sauté pan until hot. Gently sauté the onion and mushrooms until the onions are soft and golden brown.

In the meantime, combine the milk and Parmesan cheese. Stir thoroughly; set aside.

Add the rice to the onion mixture and continue stirring for approximately 5 minutes until all excess moisture has been absorbed and the grains of rice are thoroughly coated. Increasing the heat, carefully add the wine and continue stirring until the mixture becomes syrupy.

Continue stirring and adding approximately 1 cup of the stock at a time, until all the liquid is absorbed, Add the milk/cheese mixture as well as the asparagus and sun-dried tomatoes. Cook for several minutes. Turn off the heat and add the saffron, again stirring well. Serve in heated bowls.   Makes 4 to 6 generous servings.

Serve with a Sémillon.

Risotto Milanese

½ cup olive oil	½ teaspoon powdered saffron
1 large onion, chopped	Salt and pepper
4 cloves garlic, chopped	½ cup dried Italian mushrooms
1 ½ cups long grain or arborio	(softened in hot water,
rice	drained and chopped)
4 ½ cups boiling chicken broth	1 ½ cups grated Parmesan
1 ½ cups Chardonnay wine	cheese

Heat oil in heavy pan, add the onion and garlic. Sauté until soft. Add rice, stirring constantly until rice is golden.

Add 2 cups broth, stirring as broth is absorbed. Add more broth, a cup at a time, and stir until absorbed. Add wine; stir.

Stir in saffron, salt, pepper and softened mushrooms. When all liquid is absorbed and the rice is tender, stir in cheese.   Serves 6.

Serve with a Chardonnay.

Quick Risotto

2 cups arborio rice	¼ cup Chardonnay wine
2 cups water	Salt and pepper
1 ½ to 2 cups hot chicken stock	1 tablespoon chopped parsley
½ cup grated Parmesan cheese	1 tablespoon chopped basil

Place rice and water in saucepan and bring to a boil. Boil for 5 minutes. Drain rice and spread on a baking sheet. (May be completed to this point the day before.)

When ready to complete, place rice back in a saucepan. Slowly add chicken stock, ½ cup at a time while stirring, until rice is tender but not mushy. Add the cheese and wine; continue to stir. Season with salt and pepper. Fold in herbs.   Serves 8.

Serve with a Chardonnay.

Linguine with Smoked Chicken, Sun-Dried Tomatoes, Basil & Roasted Garlic

3 shallots, finely diced
2 tablespoons olive oil
1 cup beef stock
1 cup Cabernet Sauvignon
  wine
½ cup cream
1 cup diced smoked chicken
¼ cup sliced sun-dried
  tomatoes
¼ cup pitted and chopped
  kalamata olives

¼ cup Roasted Garlic Cloves
  (recipe follows)
1 pound linguine, cooked
  according to package
  instructions
Salt and pepper
¼ cup chopped fresh basil
Asiago cheese, finely grated

Sauté shallots in olive oil for 5 minutes. Add beef stock and wine to saucepan and reduce by half. Add cream and simmer to thicken. Add chicken, tomatoes, olives and Roasted Garlic Cloves. Pour over pasta. Season to taste with salt and pepper.

Garnish with fresh basil and grated Asiago cheese.   Serves 4.

ROASTED GARLIC CLOVES:
In a small baking dish, roast 8 to 10 whole garlic cloves with 1 tablespoon olive oil in a 350 degree oven for 30 minutes or until golden.

Serve with a Cabernet Sauvignon.

75

Strawberry Risotto Champenoise

This is an ethereal dish with subtle, savory flavors. The strawberries add a beautiful touch of color, aroma and flavor, but no sweetness. It is essential that the Champagne be dry, and of excellent quality.

½ cup Strawberry Purée
  (recipe follows)
5 to 6 cups homemade
  chicken broth
4 tablespoons unsalted
  butter
½ cup minced onion

1 ½ cups arborio rice
  (available at specialty and
  Italian markets)
1 cup Champagne (Brut)
¼ cup Mascarpone (a soft,
  slightly sweet Italian cheese)
  or softened cream cheese

Prepare Strawberry Purée and set aside.

STRAWBERRY PURÉE:
Wash and trim fresh berries to make 1 cup. Reserve a few for garnish. (If you can procure fraises des bois, the tiny aromatic wild strawberries that have a creamy yellow flesh, so much the better.) Purée the strawberries in a food processor or blender and set aside. Slice reserved berries.

Bring broth to a simmer in saucepan. In a heavy flameproof saucepan or handled casserole, melt 3 tablespoons of the butter. When butter begins to bubble, add minced onion and sauté until soft. Do not allow onion to brown. Reduce heat to low.

Add rice to onion mixture. Mix and turn with a wooden spoon to coat the grains with butter, 1 to 2 minutes. Stirring constantly, add ½ cup of the Champagne. When the liquid is absorbed, add ½ cup of the hot broth and continue stirring. When liquid is almost completely absorbed, add ½ cup more broth. Stirring frequently, continue adding ½ cup broth, keeping heat low enough so there is about 2 minutes between additions.

When the rice has been cooking for approximately 18 minutes, add the Strawberry Purée and mix while continuing to stir and add the remaining broth.

When rice is al dente (tender but firm), approximately 20 minutes, stir in remaining ½ cup Champagne, remaining tablespoon of butter and the Mascarpone.

Serve at once in warm dishes or soup bowls, each garnished with a sliced strawberry.   Makes 4 to 6 servings.

Serve with a Champagne (Brut).

Bow Tie Pasta with Hazelnut Cheese Sauce

1 package (8 ounces) bow tie
  pasta
½ cup chopped hazelnuts
¼ cup pinenuts
1 tablespoon butter
1 tablespoon olive oil
½ cup white wine

½ cup crumbled blue cheese
Salt and pepper
¼ cup shredded Parmesan
  cheese
2 tablespoons snipped fresh
  basil

Cook pasta in boiling water according to package directions; drain. Return to pan and keep warm.

Meanwhile, in a medium skillet, cook the nuts in the butter and oil, stirring frequently, until nuts are toasted and butter begins to brown. Add the wine and blue cheese, stirring to blend the cheese. Stir nut mixture into the pasta. Toss gently to coat; salt and pepper to taste.

Serve sprinkled with the Parmesan cheese and fresh basil.
                                                        Serves 4.

Serve with a Pinot Blanc or Reisling.

Smoked Salmon Fettuccine

2 cloves garlic, minced
1 cup sliced fresh mushrooms
½ red bell pepper, sliced into
  thin strips
1 cup diced fresh tomatoes
8 ounces smoked salmon
  slices, cut into small pieces
6 tablespoons virgin olive oil
½ cup Dry Vermouth
½ cup finely chopped fresh
  parsley

½ cup finely sliced green
  onions, including part of
  green top
1 teaspoon dried oregano
2 teaspoons fresh chopped
  basil
1 teaspoon dried thyme
1 cup half-and-half
12 ounces fresh fettuccine
½ cup grated Parmesan
  cheese

In a medium skillet, cook the garlic, mushrooms, peppers, tomatoes and smoked salmon in the olive oil over medium heat for about 5 minutes. Add Vermouth. Stir in the parsley, green onions and herbs. Add half-and-half and simmer for 3 to 5 minutes while pasta is cooking.

Cook pasta according to package directions, or until al dente, stirring frequently. Drain.

Pour drained fettuccine into a large bowl, cover with sauce and toss. Sprinkle with grated cheese. Serve with a green salad and French bread.   Serves 4.

Serve with a Fumé Blanc or Sauvignon Blanc.

Meats

COOKING WITH WINE

Pan Seared Beef Tenderloin with a Caramelized Shallot and Fig Sauce

2 tablespoons sugar
3 tablespoons butter
8 medium shallots, peeled
1 cup veal stock, or canned
  beef broth
2 cups Cabernet Sauvignon
  wine

2 allspice berries
¼ head of fennel, shaved
1 tablespoon chopped fresh
  thyme
¼ teaspoon whole black
  peppercorns
4 fresh figs

In an oven-proof saucepan or heavy gauge sauté pan, melt the sugar to a golden caramel. Stir in 2 tablespoons of the butter. Add shallots and coat them with the mixture. Add the veal stock and bring to a boil. Place the pan in a 350 degree oven for approximately 1 hour, or until the shallots have become soft. Remove from oven and return to high heat. Reduce the juice to a syrup. Cool and slice shallots, then set aside.

In another pan reduce the wine with the spices and herbs. Reduce to about ⅔ cup. Strain out herbs and spices. Add the caramelized shallots and syrup to the strained wine reduction. Set aside.

BEEF TENDERLOIN:
Salt and pepper
1 ¼ pounds center-cut beef
  tenderloin

1 sprig fresh thyme, chopped
1 tablespoon cooking oil
1 tablespoon butter

Salt and pepper the trimmed beef, then sprinkle with the thyme. Heat a large cast iron skillet over medium high heat. Add the cooking oil and heat close to smoking. Add the meat and butter. Brown the meat on all sides, and cook to the desired serving temperature. Remove and let rest five minutes.

Place the sauce back on the stove and add the fresh figs. Bring to a simmer. Remove from heat and stir in the remaining tablespoon of butter. Distribute sauce between 4 plates. Slice the beef loin and place directly on the sauce. Serve and enjoy. This may be served with grilled polenta.   Serves 4.

Serve with a Cabernet Sauvignon.

Beef Stew Burgundy

5 medium onions, sliced thin
2 tablespoons bacon drippings
3 pounds lean beef stew meat,
  cut in 1-inch cubes
1 ½ tablespoons flour
Salt and pepper
1 tablespoon chopped thyme

1 tablespoon chopped
  marjoram
2 cups beef broth
1 cup Merlot wine
½ pound fresh mushrooms,
  sliced

In heavy skillet, sauté onions in bacon drippings until brown. Remove onions from pan and set aside. Add meat and brown in same pan. When browned, sprinkle with flour, salt, pepper, thyme and marjoram; toss well.

Add broth and wine; mix well. Simmer for 3 ½ hours. (Add additional broth and wine as needed to keep meat barely covered.)

Return onions to skillet and add the mushrooms to simmer during the last hour of cooking or until meat is tender.

Serve with rice, noodles or polenta. This stew has a very rich and robust flavor. Serves 8.

Serve with a Merlot or a Carignan.

Entrecote al Queso Cabralesso
(Beef Steak in a Blue Cheese Sauce)

¼ pound sharp blue cheese
  (Oregon or Danish Blue)
1 cup Champagne (Brut)
3 tablespoons butter
½ cup heavy cream
2 large cloves garlic, minced
1 pound wild mushrooms
  (shiitake, oyster, brown)

½ teaspoon ground nutmeg
6 steaks (8 ounces each)
¾ teaspoon coarsely ground
  black pepper
1 teaspoon salt
1 ½ cups brown veal stock

To prepare the sauce, place blue cheese and ¾ cup of the Champagne in a bowl; cream with a fork. Melt 1 tablespoon of the butter in a pan; add cheese/wine mixture and cream. Bring to a boil and reduce by ⅓, stirring. Set aside.

Heat remaining 2 tablespoons butter in a skillet. Over low heat, sauté garlic until soft and golden; add mushrooms, nutmeg and the remaining Champagne. Cook until mushrooms start to wilt, 6 to 8 minutes. Transfer to the pan with the cheese sauce.

Shortly before serving time, season both sides of each steak with pepper. Heat a heavy skillet, which is large enough to hold the steaks, until very hot. Sprinkle salt in the skillet and add steaks. Cook the meat quickly over high heat -- it shouldn't burn, but should get dark brown, about 5 minutes on each side depending on thickness. The steaks should be rare, as they will continue to cook for a few minutes after they are removed from the heat. Transfer meat to a cutting board and let rest for about 5 minutes.

Meanwhile, pour veal stock into the skillet where the meat cooked. Over high heat, stir and scrape the bottom and sides of the skillet with a spatula to loosen all the browned bits of meat. Cook until reduced to about ½ cup. Pour contents into the pan with the mushroom sauce. Stir and taste for seasoning.   Serves 6 to 8.

Serve the steak with the delicious cheese and mushroom sauce and a Champagne (Brut).

Pork Scallops with Dijon Sauce

1 tablespoon butter
1 tablespoon vegetable oil
1 ¼ pound lean pork scallops
½ cup dry white wine

½ cup chicken broth
1 cup heavy cream
1 teaspoon Dijon mustard

Divide butter and oil into 2 large, heavy skillets over medium heat. Arrange the scallops so they do not overlap in the pan. If crowded, they will steam rather than brown. Cook for 1 minute, or until brown. Transfer to a plate and keep warm. Discard the fat from the skillets.

Add half of the broth to each skillet. Cook over high heat, scraping bits from the bottom. Combine liquid into 1 skillet.

To the skillet with the broth, add the wine. Boil until reduced, about 5 minutes. Remove from heat and whisk in the cream and mustard. Pour over scallops. Wild rice or thinly sliced roasted potatoes go well with this dish.   Serves 6.

Serve with Chardonnay.

Beef Tenderloin with Caramelized Onions

1 tablespoon butter	2 pounds beef tenderloin
2 large yellow onions, sliced thin	1 teaspoon olive oil
	Salt and pepper
1 clove garlic	¼ cup Port wine

In a heavy skillet, heat the butter over medium heat. Mound the onion slices in the pan; they will cook down considerably. Cook gently for 45 minutes to an hour, occasionally turning over the onions to keep them from burning. They will turn a rich caramel color.

While the onions are cooking, prepare the beef. Cut the garlic into 6 slivers, and insert at intervals in the sides of the tenderloin using a small, sharp knife. Coat the beef lightly with olive oil, and a few sprinkles of salt and pepper.

Roast the beef tenderloin in a 425 degree oven for 20 minutes, or until it reads 135 degrees on a meat thermometer. Remove to a carving board and keep in a warm place.

When the onions are caramelized, add the Port and simmer a few minutes to combine. Salt and pepper to taste. Slice the beef tenderloin and serve topped with the caramelized onions.

Serves 6 to 8.

Serve with a Cabernet Sauvignon or Pinot Noir.

Beef Burgundy

Marinating the meat as indicated in the recipe is very important to achieve the depth of flavor.

2 pounds stew beef, cut into 1 ½-inch cubes	1 carrot, scraped and sliced
1 medium onion, sliced	1 clove garlic, minced
2 cups red wine	3 tablespoons butter
4 sprigs fresh parsley, or 2 tablespoons dried	1 tablespoon flour
¼ teaspoon thyme	½ cup beef broth
2 tablespoons cooking oil	1 bay leaf
½ teaspoon salt	¼ pound salt pork, diced
¼ teaspoon pepper	24 small white onions, peeled
	1 cup sliced fresh mushrooms

Combine the beef, onion, wine, parsley, thyme, oil, salt, pepper, carrot and garlic in a bowl. Let stand for at least 4 hours, turning meat from time to time.

Remove meat and pat dry with paper towels. Strain and reserve marinade.

In a stockpot, brown meat in 2 tablespoons of the butter. Add flour and cook for 3 minutes, stirring. Add broth and reserved marinade and bring to boil. Put in bay leaf. Cover, turn down heat, and simmer for 2 hours, stirring from time to time. Remove bay leaf.

Melt remaining 1 tablespoon butter in small saucepan. Add salt pork and small white onions. Cook over medium heat about 10 minutes, or until golden. Transfer salt pork and small white onions to the stockpot. Add mushrooms and bring to boil. Cover, turn down heat, and simmer 45 minutes longer, or until meat is tender. Serve with boiled potatoes or noodles.   Serves 8.

A Cabernet Sauvignon, Gamay Beaujolais or Barbera are ideal with this dish.

Burgundian Stew

3 tablespoons olive oil
¼ pound salt pork, diced
3 pounds gourmet beef stew
  meat, cut into 1-inch cubes
Flour
Salt and pepper
3 medium onions, diced
2 cloves garlic, minced
2 cups dry red wine
1 cup beef broth

1 bay leaf
3 tablespoons chopped fresh
  parsley
2 tablespoons minced chervil
1 teaspoon thyme
1 tablespoon tarragon vinegar
6 carrots, sliced
½ pound mushrooms, sliced
1 tablespoon butter

Heat olive oil in a heavy saucepan. Add salt pork. Sprinkle beef cubes with flour seasoned with salt and pepper. Sear meat thoroughly in the hot fat.

Add onions and garlic. Cook until onions are yellow. Add the wine, beef broth, bay leaf, parsley, chervil, thyme and vinegar. Cover and simmer for 1 ¼ hours until meat is tender.

Remove bay leaf. Add sliced carrots. Cover and cook 30 minutes longer. Meanwhile sauté mushrooms in butter. Add to stew after carrots are tender.

Sprinkle with fresh chopped parsley. Serve with buttered egg noodles. Serves 8 to 10.

A Burgundy, Pinot Noir, or Barbera will go well with this stew.

Fillet of Beef with Bleu Cheese, Rosemary and Pine Nut Sauce

6 beef tenderloin portions
(4 ounces each)
Salt and freshly ground black
pepper
2 tablespoons olive oil
2 shallots, minced
1 tablespoon butter

½ cup Cabernet Sauvignon
wine
2 cups veal stock
1 tablespoon rosemary
4 tablespoons crumbled bleu
cheese
½ cup toasted pine nuts

Lightly pound the meat to flatten. Season both sides with salt and pepper. Sear in the olive oil over high heat in a non-reactive, stainless steel pan. Turn over and sear on the other side. Remove to a plate and keep warm while making the sauce.

Pour off any excess oil and sauté shallots in butter to soften. Deglaze with wine and reduce to almost dry. Add veal stock and rosemary; reduce to a sauce consistency. Finish with bleu cheese and any juices that have run out of the meat. Spoon sauce over meat and garnish with chopped toasted pine nuts.   Serves 6

Enjoy with a glass of Cabernet Sauvignon.

Stuffed Roast Pork

6 dried prunes, roughly
  chopped
6 dried apricots, roughly
  chopped
½ cup golden raisins
6 toasted pecans, chopped
3 cloves garlic, chopped

1 cup of Merlot wine
2 pork tenderloins
  (approximately 1 to 1 ½
  pounds each)
Salt and pepper
6 apples
6 medium onions, peeled

Combine the prunes, apricots, raisins, pecans, and garlic in a small bowl. Add the wine and set aside to soak. Preheat oven to 350 degrees.

Make a lengthwise cut in the pork tenderloins, but do not cut all the way through. Flatten slightly with the side of a cleaver or a rolling pin. Spread the fruit and nut mixture over the tenderloins and season with salt and pepper. Roll the roasts and tie with string. Season the outside liberally with salt and pepper.

Roast for 30 minutes per pound, surrounded with apples and onions. (The apples and onions may be roasted in the same oven but in a separate pan, if you do not want them to roast in the fatty juices released by the pork.)

To serve, slice the pork tenderloins into 1-inch thick slices. Place on plates with the pan-roasted apples and onions, and mashed sweet potatoes.   Serves 4 to 6.

Serve with a Merlot.

Pork Loin Roast Chardonnay

1 trimmed pork loin, 3 to 4 pounds	1 teaspoon paprika
2 teaspoons prepared mustard	1 clove garlic, crushed
Salt and pepper	1 small onion, grated
½ teaspoon caraway seeds	¾ cup Chardonnay wine

Rub the roast with mustard, salt and pepper. Then, season with caraway seeds, paprika, garlic and onion. Place the roast in a dish and add the wine. Let it marinate for several hours before cooking. Remove the roast, strain the marinade, and set marinade aside.

Preheat oven to 300 degrees. Place the roast in a covered pan and pour marinade over the roast. Cook for 2 ½ to 3 hours, basting occasionally. Add water and more wine if the juices dry up too quickly.   Serves 8.

Serve with a Chardonnay.

Barbecued Butterflied Leg of Lamb

1 leg of lamb (5 pounds)

MARINADE:	½ cup roughly chopped fresh rosemary
1 cup olive oil	4 cloves garlic, minced
¼ cup soy sauce or Worcestershire sauce	1 cup red wine
1 cup chopped fresh mint	Salt and pepper

Have the butcher butterfly the leg of lamb. Combine the marinade ingredients in a large bowl. Place the lamb fat-side up in the bowl, so that the marinade is in contact with the meat. Marinate for 6 hours or overnight, turning several times.

Grill over a medium-hot fire, turning several times, until tender and slightly pink inside. Slice and serve with sautéed polenta squares and ratatouille.   Serves 6 to 8.

Serve with a Merlot or Cabernet Sauvignon.

Roasted Pork Tenderloin with Lavender and Mint

⅔ cup finely chopped fresh mint
2 tablespoons coarsely chopped dried lavender
2 teaspoons finely minced fresh garlic
4 tablespoons soy sauce
2 tablespoons freshly squeezed orange juice
2 tablespoons olive oil

⅓ cup Merlot wine
2 pork tenderloins, (10 ounces each) trimmed of all fat and silverskin
½ teaspoon salt
½ teaspoon fresh ground pepper
2 tablespoons canola or safflower oil

Mix mint, lavender, garlic, soy sauce, orange juice, olive oil and wine together. Add pork, coating all sides. Cover and marinate in refrigerator overnight. Remove pork from marinade and wipe off most of the herbs and spices. Discard marinade.

Preheat oven to 450 degrees. Season each pork tenderloin with about ½ teaspoon of salt and pepper. In a hot pan that has been lightly oiled with the canola oil, sear meat on all sides.

Remove pork to oven-proof pan or dish. Put in oven for 12 to 20 minutes or until meat is just cooked through. Take out and let meat rest, loosely covered, for 3 to 4 minutes. Slice thinly and serve with a spicy peach chutney.   Serves 6 to 8.

Serve with a Merlot.

Lamb Curry

¼ cup olive oil
¼ cup butter
2 large onions, minced
3 to 4 pounds lean lamb, cut in
  1 to 2-inch cubes
2 cloves garlic, crushed
1 teaspoon salt
1 teaspoon coarsely ground
  black pepper

1 cup chicken broth
1 ½ cups Sweet Vermouth
1 tablespoon cornstarch or
  arrowroot
3 tablespoons curry powder
3 tablespoons water

Heat oil and butter in large, heavy skillet. Sauté onions until browned. Add meat; sauté 20 minutes. Add garlic, salt, pepper, broth and Vermouth. Bring to a boil; lower heat and simmer, covered, for 1 hour.

Make a paste of cornstarch, curry powder and water. Blend paste thoroughly into the meat mixture. Continue simmering for 5 to 10 minutes, until liquid is slightly thickened.

Serve over steamed rice, accompanied by such condiments as chutney, shredded coconut, chopped peanuts, raisins and fresh mango, if available.   Serves 6 to 8.

Best served with a Cabernet Sauvignon.

Medallions of Lamb with Black Olive Tapenade

From France's Provence region, Tapenade is a thick paste which is used as a condiment.

6 lamb loins, approximately ½ pound each
2 tablespoons olive oil
6 teaspoons chopped fresh thyme
6 teaspoons chopped fresh rosemary
2 teaspoons minced garlic
1 tablespoon butter

½ cup Cabernet Sauvignon wine
1 cup lamb or beef stock
¼ cup tomato purée
2 tablespoons Tapenade (recipe follows)
Salt and pepper
Thyme or rosemary sprigs for garnish

Rub the lamb loins with olive oil. Season each loin with 1 teaspoon of the thyme and 1 teaspoon of the rosemary. Marinate for at least one hour prior to grilling.

Sauté the garlic in butter; add wine and reduce to 1 tablespoon. Add the stock and tomato purée, and reduce to 1 cup. Add Tapenade, salt and pepper. Set aside.

Grill lamb loins for 6 to 10 minutes or until medium rare. Slice and serve over warm sauce. Garnish with thyme or rosemary sprigs.

Serves 6.

TAPENADE:
1 can (6 ounces) pitted black olives (preferably Greek)
1 ounce anchovy fillets
1 clove garlic, minced

2 tablespoons capers
2 tablespoons olive oil
2 tablespoons lemon juice
Pepper

Put all ingredients except pepper in a food processor. Process to a coarse chop. Transfer to a bowl, and add pepper to taste. Store in refrigerator.

Makes 1 cup.

Serve with a Cabernet Sauvignon.

Savory Herbed Rack of Lamb

½ cup Merlot wine
¼ cup balsamic vinegar
¼ cup soy sauce
2 heaping tablespoons Dijon
  mustard
2 heaping teaspoons minced
  fresh garlic
½ teaspoon rosemary

½ teaspoon oregano
½ teaspoon marjoram
½ teaspoon thyme
2 tablespoons olive oil
2 racks of lamb, cleaned and
  trimmed of all fat and
  silverskin
1 tablespoon oil

Put the wine, vinegar, soy sauce, mustard, garlic, rosemary, oregano, marjoram, thyme and olive oil into a large glass or non-reactive dish; mix well. Add lamb and marinate at least 2 hours or overnight.

Preheat oven to 450 degrees. Heat heavy sauté pan and put in oil. Remove racks from marinade; discard marinade. Sear meat on all sides until nicely browned. Place in oven 8 to 12 minutes for medium rare. Remove from oven and let rest for 2 to 4 minutes.

Slice lamb into chops and serve. Serves 8.

Delicious with a Merlot or Grenache.

Braised Lamb Shank with Roasted Vegetables

4 lamb shanks (have butcher level off meat end on band saw)
4 cups lamb stock
1 cup Cabernet Sauvignon wine
12 baby carrots, peeled
12 baby turnips, peeled

12 garlic cloves, peeled
12 baby beets
12 pearl onions
2 tablespoons olive oil
1 cup barley, cooked in light lamb stock
1 tablespoon butter
1 bunch fresh mint

Trim, season and brown the shanks. Add lamb stock to cover ⅔ of the meat. Cover directly on top of meat with aluminum foil and reduce heat to low; turn every 20 minutes and keep level of stock at half way. Cook approximately 2 to 3 hours.

While the shanks are cooking, reduce the wine to a light syrup. When the lamb is done, strain 1 ½ cups of the cooking liquid into the wine. Simmer for 15 minutes, and skim off fat. Strain again and adjust seasoning with salt and pepper.

In a roasting pan, lightly brown carrots, turnips and garlic. Cover and roast at 400 degrees until done. In a separate pan, toss the beets and onions in olive oil and salt and pepper. Roast, uncovered, until done. Cool, then peel.

For presentation, warm the lamb. Stand each shank in the center of a plate and surround with the wine sauce which has been combined with the cooked barley. Toss the vegetables in a little fresh butter and mint leaves. Place around the lamb.   Serves 4.

Serve with a Cabernet Sauvignon or Merlot.

Curried Lamb

¼ cup golden raisins
Salt and pepper
2 pounds lamb stew meat from the leg or shoulder, cut into 1-inch cubes
1 tablespoon vegetable oil
2 white onions, peeled and sliced
1 carrot, peeled and diced
2 shallots, peeled and chopped
1 ½ teaspoons whole cumin seed
1 teaspoon anise seed
2 whole cloves
½ teaspoon ground black pepper

1 ½ tablespoons of a good quality curry powder
½ cup Sauvignon Blanc wine
2 cups unsalted chicken stock
⅓ cup chopped almonds, lightly toasted
1 medium potato, peeled, diced and set aside in water
4 tablespoons cornstarch
¾ cup light cream (half-and-half)
¼ cup heavy cream
Salt and pepper
Chopped chervil for garnish

In a small bowl, soak the raisins in warm water to cover. Set aside. Preheat oven to 350 degrees. Salt and pepper the lamb well on all sides. In a large heavy pot, heat the vegetable oil until very hot. Brown the lamb in batches, being careful not to cover the entire bottom of the pot. Remove meat from pot and set aside.

In the same pot, sauté the onions, carrot and shallots for several minutes over medium-high heat, stirring regularly, until they begin to soften and brown slightly. Add the spices and stir for another minute. Deglaze the pot with wine and stir to bubble off the browned bits and meat juices. Return meat to pot, add chicken stock and almonds; bring rapidly to a boil. Cover pot tightly and transfer to oven. Braise for 45 minutes. Stir in potato, and return to oven, covered, for another 45 minutes or until meat is tender.

Remove pot from oven. With a slotted spoon, remove meat and set aside. With a ladle or large spoon, remove as much fat as possible from the sauce. Reduce cooking juices, if necessary. Whisk together cornstarch and ½ cup of the light cream. Whip into simmering sauce to thicken lightly (you may not need all the cornstarch mixture).

Add the remaining light cream and the heavy cream, and adjust texture. Stir in drained raisins and meat, and warm through gently. Taste and season with salt and pepper. Serve with fluffy basmati rice. Garnish with chervil. Serves 4 to 6.

A Sauvignon Blanc or Grenache are suggested.

Sherried Kidney Sauté

4 lamb kidneys	Salt and pepper
1 medium onion, chopped fine	1 cup Dry Sherry
2 tablespoons butter	Chopped fresh parsley
12 fresh mushrooms, sliced	

Cut kidneys in half; remove any fat and outer membrane. Cut kidneys into ½-inch slices. Cover with cold, salted water and let stand for 1 hour. Drain and rinse kidneys thoroughly with fresh running water. Drain.

Sauté the onion in melted butter; add kidneys and mushrooms. Sauté until kidneys are nicely browned.

Add salt and pepper to taste. Add Sherry. Simmer in a covered pan for 5 to 10 minutes over low heat until kidneys are tender. Sprinkle with fresh chopped parsley and serve over toast. Serves 2.

Good with a Cabernet Sauvignon.

Veal Sauté with Mushrooms

2 large white or yellow onions, finely chopped
1 cup chopped parsley
1 clove garlic, peeled and minced
½ pound fresh mushrooms, sliced
2 sprigs fresh rosemary or ¼ teaspoon dried
2 sprigs fresh oregano or ¼ teaspoon dried

¼ cup olive oil
2 pounds top round veal steak, sliced into ½ × ½ × 1 ½-inch strips
1 teaspoon salt
¼ teaspoon ground black pepper
½ cup sliced green olives
1 cup white wine
⅛ teaspoon allspice
1 slice of lemon

Sauté onions, parsley, garlic, mushrooms, rosemary and oregano in heated olive oil until slightly cooked but not browned. Add veal strips, salt and pepper. Sauté slightly, about 5 minutes, mixing well.

Add olives, wine, allspice and lemon. Cover and simmer until veal is tender, 10 to 15 minutes. Discard lemon slice. Serve with egg noodles cooked "al dente", and a tossed salad.   Serves 6.

Serve with a Zinfandel or Gewürztraminer.

Baked Pork Chops with Cabernet Sauvignon

8 very lean, center cut pork chops, cut ½-inch thick
2 to 3 eggs (can use whites only)
3 tablespoons chopped fresh parsley
Salt and pepper
2 cups seasoned bread crumbs (very fine)
6 medium yellow onions, peeled and sliced
3 bell peppers, seeded and sliced julienne
6 cloves garlic, minced
¼ cup water
¼ balsamic vinegar
1 cup Cabernet Sauvignon wine

Preheat oven to 350 degrees. Trim chops of any residual fat. Beat eggs in large bowl, add parsley, salt and pepper. Dip each chop in egg, cover with bread crumbs.

Place chops on an oiled cookie sheet and bake until brown. Do not over cook, as they will bake for an additional 2 hours at 250 degrees. When browned, set aside.

Prepare a large glass baking dish. Arrange ⅓ of the onions and peppers on bottom of dish. Place a layer of chops on top. Sprinkle garlic on top of chops. Then repeat onions and peppers; top with chops and minced garlic. Then top again with remaining onions and peppers.

Combine water, vinegar and wine; pour over chops. Season with salt and pepper. Cover with foil and bake for 2 hours at 250 degrees.

Check every 35 to 40 minutes, adding some wine if needed, and turn chops. Cover and return to oven. You will notice a marvelous aroma as the vinegar, wine, onion, and pepper flavors blend. Uncover for the last 15 minutes to allow the liquid to reduce and thicken. Serve with steamed rice.   Serves 8.

A Cabernet Sauvignon is suggested for this dish.

Herbed Lamb

1 leg of lamb (3 pounds)	½ cup olive oil
¼ cup fresh rosemary leaves	¼ cup coarse mustard
¼ cup fresh oregano leaves	Zest of lemon
4 fresh mint leaves	1 tablespoon cracked pepper
1 cup Pinot Noir wine	1 teaspoon sea salt
1 cup light soy sauce	

Have the butcher butterfly the leg of lamb, making sure that the thickest parts are no more than 2 inches thick. Coarsely chop the herbs (or cut with scissors) into 1-inch chunks. Mix with remaining ingredients in a large bowl.

Place the lamb in the bowl fat side up, so that the meat is in contact with the juices. Marinate for at least 4 hours, but preferably overnight in the refrigerator. Strain the marinade; reduce over high heat while the lamb is cooking.

Grill the lamb over a hot fire, turning several times, until done but still pink. Let rest 15 minutes before carving. Add any meat juices to the reduced marinade.

Serve the lamb with mixed grilled vegetables, black pepper pasta and caramelized onions. Top the lamb with the reduced wine/herb sauce.   Serves 6.

Serve with a Pinot Noir.

Saltimbocca alla Roma

12 veal scaloppine
12 paper-thin slices prosciutto*
12 fresh sage leaves, or 1
   tablespoon dried

6 tablespoons butter
¾ cup Chardonnay wine
Fresh sage for garnish

Layer each scaloppine with one slice prosciutto and top with one sage leaf, or a pinch of dried sage. Fasten each together with a toothpick by making a "stitch" through the leaf and meats.

Melt butter over medium heat in a sauté pan. Sauté each scaloppine for 2 minutes on the veal side. Turn and sauté for 1 minute on the prosciutto side. Transfer to a heated platter and keep warm.

Pour wine into the sauté pan and reduce over high heat for 2 minutes. Pour over scaloppine and serve, garnished with fresh sage.   Serves 6.

*Prosciutto, an Italian ham, is available in gourmet and Italian markets and most supermarkets. It is sold in transparently thin slices.

Serve with a Chardonnay.

Meats

Veal Medallions with Chanterelle Sauce

8 slices veal scaloppine, cut
½-inch thick (approximately 2
pounds)*
3 tablespoons extra virgin olive
oil
1 large red bell pepper, cored,
seeded and julienned
6 cloves garlic, peeled

12 ounces Chanterelles,
shiitake or other seasonal
mushrooms, lightly brushed
to clean and sliced about ¼-
inch thick
¼ cup balsamic vinegar
¾ cup white wine

Heat a large skillet over high heat. Add olive oil and sauté veal 3 to
4 minutes. Lower heat slightly if oil becomes too hot and spatters.
Turn the veal and sauté 2 minutes on second side. Remove to
platter, cover with foil and keep in a 150 degree oven while sautéing
the vegetables.

Lower the heat to medium-high. In the same skillet, sauté the bell
pepper, garlic and mushrooms for 3 to 4 minutes. Add vinegar and
wine; continue cooking until liquid is reduced and slightly thickened.
Add any juice drained from veal onto the platter and reduce slightly.
Pour sauce with vegetables over medallions and serve. Serves 8.

*Ask your butcher to cut the slices from the frozen block of veal
used for scaloppine.

Serve with a Sauvignon Blanc.

Merlot Meat Loaf

1 cup coarse bread crumbs
¾ cup Merlot wine
2 pounds ground beef
1 pound ground pork
1 large onion, finely chopped
4 cloves garlic, minced
1 cup chopped stuffed green
  olives

½ cup tomato paste
2 teaspoons grainy French
  mustard
2 teaspoons chopped fresh
  basil
2 teaspoons chopped parsley
3 eggs, beaten
Salt and pepper

Combine bread crumbs and wine in a small bowl. Set aside.

In a mixing bowl, thoroughly combine the beef, pork, onion, garlic, olives, tomato paste, mustard, basil and parsley. Beat the eggs slightly, then add eggs and soaked bread crumbs to the meat mixture.

Form into a 4-inch thick loaf, and place in the center of a good-sized roasting pan so the meat is not touching the sides.

Bake in a 350 degree oven for 1 ½ hours, basting several times with the pan juices and additional wine, to form a crispy crust. Serve hot or at room temperature.   Serves 6 to 8.

Serve with a Merlot.

Holiday Brisket

1 beef brisket (4 to 5 pounds), all fat removed	Paprika
	Salt and pepper
Garlic powder	4 cups Pinot Noir wine

Place brisket in a deep roasting pan and generously apply garlic powder, paprika, salt and pepper, evenly coating the exterior. Place the brisket under the broiler and sear. Turn the brisket over and repeat.

Pour the wine into the roasting pan. Cover and seal the roasting pan completely with aluminum foil to hold in all the steam. Place the pan in a 350 degree oven and cook for approximately 2 to 3 hours, turning brisket and basting periodically until tender. The brisket is tender when you can easily pierce it with a fork.

Let the brisket cool down to at least room temperature and cut into thin slices against the grain. If brisket shreds while slicing, you should chill prior to cutting by placing it in the refrigerator in the roasting pan with the juices.

Skim off any excess fat after chilling. Seal with aluminum foil and reheat before serving. Place sliced brisket on a platter and spoon a generous amount of cooking juices over the top. Serves 6 to 8.

Wine suggestions: A Pinot Noir, or Chardonnay if you're not a red wine drinker.

Seafood

COOKING WITH WINE

Seared Scallops with Caramelized Pears and Leeks

2 Comice pears
1 tablespoon sugar
½ cup cold butter
2 leeks
2 tablespoons olive oil
1 shallot, minced
1 cup Sauvignon Blanc wine
Sea salt

White pepper, freshly ground
1 tablespoon chopped fresh
  thyme
8 ounces sea scallops
Black pepper, freshly ground
1 tablespoon Szechwan
  peppercorns, finely ground

Core the pears and cut them into wedges about ½-inch thick. Place the sugar in a stainless steel-lined sauté pan and heat until it begins to melt. Stir the sugar over medium heat, and when it becomes amber stir in 1 tablespoon of the cold butter, bit by bit, until it has been incorporated into the sugar. Using tongs, place the wedges of pear in the caramel sauce. Brown both cut sides of the pear over medium-high heat. Remove and allow to cool to room temperature. Reserve pears.

Cut the leeks in half lengthwise and wash under cold water. Remove the bottoms and slice on the bias, about ½-inch thick. Heat a sauté pan over medium heat and add 1 tablespoon of the olive oil and the shallot. Sauté briefly taking care not to brown the shallot. Add the leeks and sauté for 3 minutes. Add half of the wine and simmer 3 more minutes. Adjust seasoning with salt and white pepper. Add the thyme; remove from heat. Cool and reserve leeks.

Rinse the scallops under cold water, and pat them dry with a paper towel. Season with salt, black pepper and Szechwan pepper. Heat a skillet over high heat. Add the remaining 1 tablespoon olive oil and wait for it to start to smoke. Using tongs, add the scallops, placing them cut side down in the pan. Quickly add 1 teaspoon cold butter. Brown the scallops well on both sides, adding more cold butter after you have flipped them over. Remove the scallops and keep warm; wipe out the pan. Place the pan back over high heat and add the rest of the wine. Add the leeks and heat. Finally, stir in the rest of the cold butter. Present the scallops and pears on a bed of leeks and use the sauce from the pan to finish.   Serves 4.

Serve with a Sauvignon Blanc.

Salmon Fillets with Wild Mushroom Ragout

3 tablespoons butter
5 shallots, minced
18 ounces mixed mushrooms,
  (oyster, chanterelle, morel
  and cremini)
¾ cup bottled clam juice
¾ cup Chardonnay wine
3 tablespoons whipping cream

½ teaspoon chopped tarragon
Salt and white pepper
6 salmon fillets (6 to 8 ounces
  each)
Fresh lemon juice
2 tablespoons melted butter
Fresh tarragon sprigs for
  garnish

In a sauté pan, melt the butter. Add the shallots and sauté 2 minutes; add mushrooms and sauté for 8 minutes. Add clam juice and wine. Boil until liquids are almost completely reduced, about 20 minutes. (Can be made up to 6 hours ahead.) Add cream to mushrooms and boil until thickened, about 1 minute. Add tarragon and season to taste with salt and white pepper.

Preheat broiler. Brush salmon with lemon juice and melted butter. Broil, skin side down, about 6 minutes. Arrange on plates, spoon mushroom sauce over and garnish with fresh tarragon sprigs.

Serves 6.

Serve with a Chardonnay or Pinot Blanc.

Salmon Wrapped in Grape Leaves
with Lentil Ratatouille

1 ½ pounds salmon fillet, skinned and boned
6 large grape leaves, washed
Olive oil
Salt and black pepper
4 slices smoked bacon, diced
1 clove garlic, minced
1 onion, diced fine
12 sun-dried tomatoes, diced fine

1 cup dried French lentils
3 cups veal or vegetable stock
1 Japanese eggplant, diced
1 carrot, diced fine
½ red bell pepper, diced fine
2 cups Cabernet Sauvignon wine
1 tablespoon arrowroot

Cut the salmon into six 4-ounce pieces (about 2 × 2 inches). Lay the grape leaves with the shiny side down and the veins up. Generously oil, salt and pepper the leaves. You may have to use 2 or 3 leaves per salmon packet depending on size. Place a piece of salmon on a leaf and fold up into a packet. Refrigerate until ready to grill.

In a heavy pot, sauté the bacon until it begins to color. Add the garlic and onion. Sauté until soft. Add the tomatoes, lentils and stock. Simmer 20 to 25 minutes until lentils are done. Add more stock as needed to keep lentils covered. Sauté each of the remaining vegetables separately in olive oil until soft. Season with salt and black pepper. Reserve until all are cooked.

When lentils are cooked, drain and reserve liquid. Mix lentils and sautéed vegetables. Reduce lentil liquid by ⅔. Put aside.

Reduce the wine to ½ cup. Add reduced lentil liquid. Add arrowroot to thicken. Season with salt and pepper.

Grill salmon packets until done, approximately 6 to 8 minutes. Place 4 tablespoons of sauce on each plate. Mound lentils in center. Cut salmon packet on the bias and place atop lentils.   Serves 6.

Serve with a Cabernet Sauvignon.

Seafood Terrine with Tomato Saffron Sauce

¾ pound boneless white fish fillet (flounder, sea bass or sole), cut into 1-inch pieces
2 large egg whites
2 tablespoons bread crumbs
1 tablespoon fresh lemon juice
1 teaspoon Dijon mustard
1 teaspoon horseradish
1 dash Tabasco sauce
¼ cup plain low fat yogurt
⅓ pound scallops, diced

½ pound raw shrimp, shelled, deveined, and diced
⅔ cup shredded fresh spinach
1 tablespoon minced shallots
2 whole green onions, chopped
1 teaspoon fresh thyme
Worcestershire sauce
Salt and white pepper
Fresh dill sprigs for garnish

Process white fish, egg whites, bread crumbs, lemon juice, Dijon mustard, horseradish and Tabasco in a food processor with steel blade until coarsely ground. Add yogurt and process until mixture is smooth; keep cold.

In medium bowl, combine remaining ingredients except dill sprigs. Fold in white fish mixture until thoroughly blended.

Heat oven to 350 degrees. Spray eight 4-ounce soufflé cups with non-stick spray. Dust each lightly with flour and shake out excess.

Fill cups ⅔ full; place 4 cups in each of two 13 × 9-inch baking dishes. Pour boiling water in baking dishes to 1-inch depth. Cover with waxed paper. Bake until metal skewer comes out clean, 15 to 18 minutes. Remove to rack and cool. Prepare Tomato Saffron Sauce.

TOMATO SAFFRON SAUCE:
1 tablespoon olive oil
2 tablespoons finely diced shallots
8 Roma tomatoes, peeled, seeded and diced
Healthy pinch of saffron

¼ cup Chardonnay wine
1 tablespoon tomato paste
½ teaspoon orange zest (grated skin of ½ of an orange)
Salt and black pepper

Heat oil in medium saucepan over medium heat and add shallots. Cook for 3 minutes until soft. Increase heat and add tomatoes, saffron, wine, tomato paste and orange zest.

Cook quickly until slightly thickened. Season with salt and pepper to taste. Serve hot or at room temperature.

To serve, spoon 3 tablespoons Tomato Saffron Sauce onto salad plates. Loosen terrine from cup by running sharp knife around edge. Tap gently out of mold. Center terrine onto plate. Garnish with fresh sprigs of dill.   Serves 6.

Serve with a golden, crisp Chardonnay.

Mussels Steamed with Sauvignon Blanc, Shallots and Parsley

4 pounds mussels
4 shallots, minced
2 tablespoons unsalted butter
1 cup Sauvignon Blanc wine

Freshly ground black pepper
¼ cup chopped flat leaf
  parsley

Soak mussels in cold water. Scrub and remove the "beard". Discard any mussel that does not close after being tapped.

In a large sauté pan or saucepan with tight-fitting lid, sauté the shallots in the butter over medium heat until soft. Pour in the wine, turn the heat to high and bring to a boil. Boil for 3 minutes.

Add the mussels, season with pepper and cover. Steam for 5 minutes or until mussels open. Discard any that don't open. Sprinkle with parsley. Divide among four soup bowls and ladle broth over top. Enjoy with a crusty baguette and green salad.   Serves 4.

Serve with a Sauvignon Blanc.

Oven-Poached Salmon

2 pounds salmon tail end, boned but with the skin intact
3 or 4 sweet red onion slices
3 or 4 lemon slices
2 tablespoons butter
4 to 5 sprigs fresh tarragon or dill
Salt and pepper
1 cup Sauvignon Blanc wine

On a large sheet of aluminum foil, place the salmon tail so that it opens like a book. Make a "sandwich filling" of onion slices, lemon slices, butter, the fresh herbs, and salt and pepper on one side of the fish.

Close the "sandwich" so the filling is between the two sides of the salmon tail. Bring two opposite sides of the foil up and roll down onto the fish. Roll up one of the ends to make a fairly watertight pouch. Add the wine and roll up the open end of the foil packet, to enclose the fish.

Place the closed packet in a roasting pan. Bake at 425 degrees for 40 minutes or until cooked through. Serve topped with the red onions and with steamed or boiled potatoes.   Serves 4.

Serve with a Sauvignon Blanc.

Sea Bass in Parchment with Tomato/Basil Sauce

3 tablespoons olive oil
3 cups finely shredded
  Chinese cabbage
6 slices sea bass fillets (5
  ounces each), ½-inch thick
6 medium tomatoes, peeled,
  seeded and diced
1 ½ cups julienned fresh basil
  leaves

3 teaspoons chopped shallots
2 jalapeno chile peppers,
  seeded and chopped
3 tablespoons white wine
2 tablespoons sweet butter
Salt and white pepper

Cut six 12 × 16-inch sheets of baking parchment paper and fold in half. Open each one and grease one half lightly with some of the olive oil. On the other half, arrange ½ cup shredded cabbage. Top with a fish fillet.

Mix tomatoes with basil and sprinkle over fish. Season each with equal amounts of shallots, jalapenos and white wine. Drizzle with remaining olive oil and dot with butter. Salt and pepper to taste.

Fold other half of parchment over fish. Crimp and fold edges tightly to make an airtight seal. Packets can be made well ahead to this point and refrigerated for several hours.

Preheat oven to 375 degrees and warm a baking sheet. Place packets on hot baking sheet and bake for 10 to 12 minutes. Place on dinner plates and slit open at table to release the aromas.

Serves 6.

Serve with a dry white wine.

Brilliant Salmon

1 large fresh salmon fillet (tail piece) with skin on, approximately 2 pounds
½ teaspoon sesame oil
Grated zest of 1 lemon
Salt and pepper
½ cup plus 2 tablespoons dry white wine
4 teaspoons peanut or other light-flavored oil
1 white onion, peeled and cut in matchsticks
1 red bell pepper, cored, quartered and cut in matchsticks

1 to 2 medium crookneck squash, cleaned and sliced into matchsticks
2 teaspoons minced garlic
1 cup shredded napa cabbage
1 bunch fresh spinach, cleaned, stemmed and chopped (2 cups)
Salt and white pepper
1 teaspoon Vietnamese Nam Pla Sauce*
1 tablespoon toasted sesame seeds

Rub the fish with ¼ teaspoon of the sesame oil and the lemon zest. Salt and pepper lightly. Marinate salmon flesh side down in ½ cup of the white wine for 30 to 60 minutes. Remove from marinade and turn skin side up for five minutes before cooking to drain.

Preheat oven to 400 degrees. In a heavy oven-proof skillet, preferably non-stick, heat 2 teaspoons of the peanut oil until almost smoking. Place fish, skin side up, in pan to brown lightly, about 5 minutes. With a spatula, carefully detach fish if necessary and turn over. Transfer immediately to oven and roast uncovered until cooked but not flaking in the center. When fish is cooked, remove from oven, cover lightly, and keep warm.

For vegetable garnish, heat a heavy pan or wok with remaining 2 teaspoons peanut oil until almost smoking. Add onion and red pepper. Stir-fry for 1 to 2 minutes. Add squash and stir-fry another minute. Stir in garlic, the remaining 2 tablespoons of the wine and the remaining ¼ teaspoon sesame oil. Add napa cabbage and spinach last, stirring just to wilt. Turn off heat. Season well with salt, white pepper and Nam Pla sauce. Mix thoroughly.

To serve, carefully remove fish from skin with a metal spatula and separate into 4 portions. Place each piece in the center of a warm plate and surround with vegetables. Sprinkle lightly with toasted sesame seeds. Serves 4.

*Can be purchased in Oriental markets or many supermarkets.

The rich flavors of this dish marry perfectly with the clean crisp flavor of a Chardonnay.

Salmon with Herb Butter

¼ cup Chardonnay wine
Juice of 1 lemon
2 salmon fillets
1 cup cleaned and stemmed
  fresh spinach leaves

¼ cup chopped mixed fresh
  herbs (basil, mint, chives)
2 tablespoons butter, softened
Lemon for garnish

In a medium skillet, combine wine, lemon juice and enough cold water to cover salmon fillets. Bring to a boil. Add salmon fillets, turn heat down to low, and simmer for 7 minutes or until done.

Place fresh spinach in colander. Remove salmon from poaching liquid and pour liquid over spinach to wilt. Press out excess liquid.

Combine chopped herbs with softened butter. Place salmon on a bed of wilted spinach. Top with herb butter. Serve with a wedge of lemon. Serves 2.

Serve with a smooth crisp Chardonnay.

Fish and Rice Manzanillo Style

This recipe originated with the fishermen of Manzanillo, Mexico.

1 pound sea fish fillets, such
  as cod or snapper
4 tablespoons oil
2 whole garlic cloves
1 ½ cups long grain white rice
½ cup tomato sauce
1 cup chicken broth
½ cup Sauvignon Blanc wine
2 cloves garlic, minced
3 green onions, chopped

3 to 4 Spanish olives, cut into
  rings
½ teaspoon ground coriander
¾ teaspoon dried mint leaves
½ teaspoon ground cumin
1 tablespoon mild chili powder
Salt and pepper
Lime wedges
Salsa

Fry the fish quickly in the oil and remove from pan. Drop the whole garlic cloves into the hot oil and fry 1 minute. Discard garlic.

In the same pan, over low heat, slowly toast the rice until it is a light straw color. Then add tomato sauce, broth, wine, minced garlic, onions, olives, coriander, mint, cumin, chili powder and salt and pepper to taste. Stir thoroughly. Bury fish fillets so there is rice above and below them. Bring to a boil, cover tightly and adjust heat to lowest possible setting.

Simmer for 30 minutes and then remove from the heat. Let stand, covered, for 10 minutes. Serve with lime wedges and mild salsa.

Serves 4 to 6.

Serve with a Sauvignon Blanc or a dry Chenin Blanc.

Spicy Smoked Lavender Shrimp

2 scant tablespoons Spicy
  Lavender Mix (recipe follows)
2 heaping tablespoons honey
Juice of ½ lime
¼ cup Chardonnay wine

20 large shrimp, peeled and
  deveined
3 bunches lavender fire sticks*
Oil for brushing on shrimp

In a bowl, blend the Spicy Lavender Mix, honey, lime juice and wine. Add shrimp and marinate 1 hour.

Soak lavender fire sticks in water for 1 hour. Thread 4 to 5 shrimps onto each bamboo or metal skewer. Prepare barbecue with regular or mesquite charcoal. When coals are ashen and grey, place damp lavender fire sticks on top. Wait until smoke appears, brush shrimp with light coating of oil and place on hot grill. Cook 2 to 4 minutes per side, until shrimp are just done. Serves 4.

SPICY LAVENDER MIX:
2 tablespoons salt-free spicy
  pepper seasoning
2 healthy pinches salt
2 pinches super-fine sugar

⅛ teaspoon ground Lavender
  buds and flowers
⅛ teaspoon toasted ground
  cumin

Blend all Lavender Mix ingredients until well mixed.

*Lavender fire sticks are available in gourmet food stores.

Serve with a Chardonnay.

Shrimp Curry

4 tablespoons butter
3 to 4 tablespoons flour
2 cups milk
1 small onion, quartered
4 scallions, minced
2 carrots, finely diced
2 stalks celery, finely diced
1 red bell pepper, finely diced

1 tablespoon minced parsley
½ teaspoon powdered thyme
3 tablespoons curry powder
½ cup Gewürztraminer wine
1 pound small bay shrimp,
  cleaned
Salt and pepper

To make the sauce, melt the butter in a saucepan over low heat. Stir in the flour. Slowly add the milk, stirring until thickened. Place the quartered onion in the sauce and set aside over very low heat.

Steam sauté the vegetables, herbs, and curry power in the white wine and a little water until tender.

Add the shrimp and the sauce, discarding the quartered onion. Stir over medium heat until well combined and warmed through. Add salt, pepper, and additional curry powder to taste. Simmer over low heat for 10 to 15 minutes.

Serve over rice accompanied by bowls of condiments.   Serves 4.

A pleasant wine choice with this curry dish is a Gewürztraminer.

Porcupine Prawns and Angel Hair Pasta
with a Ginger-Garlic Black Bean Sauce

20 large prawns
Flour for dredging
1 egg, beaten
¼ package rice sticks, broken
  into 1 to 2-inch pieces*
8 ounces angel hair pasta
1 tablespoon butter
Salt and ground white pepper

Oil for frying
7 tablespoons Sauce (recipe
  follows)
2 cups heavy cream
3 green onions, slivered
  (green part only)
Black sesame seeds

Remove shells from prawns, leaving only the tail section of shell intact. Devein. Dredge the prawns first in the flour, then in the egg and lastly in the rice sticks. Cook pasta according to package. Toss with butter. Season with salt and white pepper. Keep warm.

Heat oil to 350 degrees. In small batches, cook shrimp for 30 seconds. Remove and drain. Prepare Sauce.

SAUCE:
1 cup minced ginger
8 large cloves garlic, minced
1 seeded serrano chile,
  minced
4 tablespoons sugar

4 tablespoons soy sauce
4 tablespoons black bean
  garlic paste*
½ cup Chardonnay wine

Mix ginger, garlic, serrano chile, sugar, soy sauce, black bean garlic paste and Chardonnay together; reserve.

Heat 7 tablespoons of the Sauce in sauté pan until just boiling. Add the heavy cream. Reduce slightly.

Twirl a mound of pasta in the center of each plate and spoon sauce around. Push five prawns per plate up against the pasta in a star pattern. Sprinkle green onion slivers and black sesame seeds over plate.   Serves 4.

*Available in the Oriental food section of most supermarkets.

Serve with a Chardonnay.

Shrimp Scampi

The secret to the dish is to not over-cook the shrimp. Remember to remove them from the pan, then make the sauce. Do not try to do it in one step.

4 tablespoons butter
¼ cup virgin olive oil
1 ½ pounds shrimp, cleaned,
  deveined
5 cloves garlic, minced

1 cup Chardonnay wine
½ cup fresh bread crumbs
  (very fine)
½ cup chopped green onions

Heat a large frying pan on high heat, melt 2 tablespoons of the butter with a small amount of the oil to prevent burning. Add shrimp. Watch very closely as the shrimp will cook quickly, 2 to 3 minutes. When shrimps turn opaque, remove from the pan and set aside.

To the pan, add the remaining 2 tablespoons butter, the rest of the oil and the garlic. Sauté until light brown. Add ½ cup of the wine. Continue to cook until liquid is reduced by half.

Add the shrimp to the sauce, stirring. Add the remaining ½ cup of wine, and sparingly sprinkle bread crumbs into the pan. The sauce will begin to thicken as you slowly add the crumbs. Sauce should be thick enough to fully coat the shrimp. Quickly remove from heat and garnish with chopped green onions. Serve with asparagus or broccoli.   Serves 6.

Serve with a Chardonnay or Sauvignon Blanc.

Grilled Prawns with Tomato/Basil Sauce

1 ¼ pounds large fresh prawns (about 12)
¼ cup olive oil
1 tablespoon minced garlic
2 tablespoons finely chopped shallots
1 ½ cups Champagne (Brut)
Juice of 1 lemon

2 tablespoons butter, cut into small pieces
5 large basil leaves (stack them up, roll like a cigar, and julienne thinly)
1 large tomato, ripe and sweet, cut into large dice
Salt and pepper

Start the coals on your grill, then peel prawn tails only, leaving head attached to tail. Lay prawns flat on plate. Pour all but 1 tablespoon olive oil over the prawns, coating well. Set aside.

Heat a 7-inch sauté pan over medium heat. Add the remaining olive oil and coat the bottom of the pan. Add the garlic and shallots. Sauté about 30 seconds. Add the Champagne and lemon juice, cooking until ¼ of the liquid has evaporated. Stir in butter and basil. Add tomatoes. Season to taste with salt and pepper. Keep warm, but do not cook to retain the fresh tomato flavor.

By now, the coals should be at their hottest. Season the prawns on both sides with salt and freshly ground black pepper. Grill for approximately 10 seconds per side on a covered grill, turning with tongs. Remove with tongs, place on dinner plates and divide the sauce between the two portions, spooning it directly over the prawn's tails.   Serves 2.

Serve with a Champagne (Brut).

Rock Shrimp with Radiatore Pasta

½ pound rock shrimp,
  deveined
1 tablespoon olive oil
1 shallot, diced
2 garlic cloves, minced
2 Roma tomatoes, chopped
1 roasted red bell pepper,
  seeded and chopped
½ cup Chardonnay wine
5 capers

Pinch of saffron
2 cups radiatore pasta, cooked
  according to package
  directions and drained
Salt and pepper
2 teaspoons butter
Juice of half of a lemon
¼ cup chopped fresh basil
Parmesan cheese, grated

Sauté the shrimp in a hot skillet in the olive oil. Add shallot, garlic, tomatoes and red pepper; sauté for 30 seconds. Add the wine, capers and saffron. Reduce to half.

Add the pasta; salt and pepper to taste. Add butter and lemon juice to finish. Toss. Top with fresh basil and Parmesan cheese.

Serves 2.

Serve with a Chardonnay.

Spicy Cajun Shrimp

4 ounces hot Cajun sausages, quartered and sliced
1 pound raw medium shrimp, peeled and deveined
2 teaspoons bacon fat (if needed)
2 shallots, finely chopped
2 teaspoons minced garlic
½ cup chopped red bell pepper

½ cup Chardonnay wine
2 tablespoons white wine vinegar (optional)
1 bay leaf
2 teaspoons tomato paste
1 cup heavy cream
Salt and freshly ground black pepper
Tabasco sauce
Chopped parsley for garnish

In a heavy skillet, brown sausages over medium heat to render fat. Remove from skillet and set aside, discarding some of the fat if necessary, but leaving 2 teaspoons in the pan. Salt shrimp evenly. Raise heat in skillet to high and cook shrimp just until they turn pink, turning once. Remove from skillet and set aside with sausages to keep warm.

There should be about 2 teaspoons of fat in pan. If necessary, add bacon fat. Sauté shallots, garlic and red bell pepper over medium-low heat for 1 to 2 minutes. Do not let brown. Deglaze pan with wine and white wine vinegar to loosen juices. Let bubble briefly, scraping bottom and sides of pan. Add bay leaf, tomato paste and cream. Simmer over low heat to thicken sauce slightly, return shrimp and sausage to sauce and heat through gently. Add salt and pepper. Sauce should be spicy. You may need a little additional Tabasco for the proper balance. Remove bay leaf.

Serve with fluffy white rice. Sprinkle with chopped parsley.

Serves 2 to 4.

A Chardonnay or Pinot Blanc is a perfect complement to this dish.

Seared Scallops with Leeks & Ginger

3 cups julienned leeks, white part only
3 tablespoons unsalted butter
¼ cup plus 4 tablespoons Gewürztraminer wine
2 pounds sea scallops
1 cup heavy cream

3 teaspoons grated fresh ginger
½ teaspoon salt
¼ teaspoon white pepper
Pinch of nutmeg
1 tablespoon safflower oil
1 tablespoon minced parsley

In a large covered pan, cook leeks in 2 tablespoons of the butter and 4 tablespoons of the wine over low heat until translucent, about 15 minutes. Uncover and remove from heat.

Peel off small side muscle attached to scallops and reserve.

Combine cream, remaining ¼ cup of the wine, ginger, salt, pepper and nutmeg in a small pan. Add side muscle trimmings and simmer. Reduce by ⅓, about 15 minutes. Strain and add to leeks.

Heat a non-stick pan over high heat. Add the remaining 1 tablespoon butter and the oil. When foam subsides, add scallops a few at a time and sear for a few seconds on each side until light brown in places. Be sure not to cook all the way through. Remove from pan and continue until all are seared.

Add scallops and cooking liquid to leeks and gently reheat until scallops are just firm to the touch (about 1 minute). Garnish with parsley.   Serve 4.

Serve with a Gewürztraminer.

Sea Scallop Surprise

6 sheets phyllo dough (10 × 14 inches each)
Melted butter
1 pound fresh sea scallops (halve the large ones)

Fresh lemon juice
Softened butter
Salt and white pepper
Red Pepper Sauce (recipe follows)

Preheat oven to 400 degrees. Lay out one sheet of phyllo at a time. (Keep remainder covered with plastic wrap to prevent drying.) Brush sheet with melted butter. Bring two 10-inch edges together. Brush again with melted butter. Divide the scallops into six portions, about 1 ½ ounces each. Place one portion along the 10-inch edge closest to you, leaving 1 ½ inches free on either end. Sprinkle scallops with lemon juice, dot with softened butter and sprinkle with salt and pepper. Roll up, starting with scallop edge. Twist ends in opposite directions to enclose filling. (It should look like a party "snapper.") Place on a cookie sheet. When all are formed, bake for 10 minutes.

RED PEPPER SAUCE:
2 large fresh sweet red bell peppers

¾ cup Champagne (Brut)
½ cup sour cream

Roast peppers over an open flame or under broiler until charred on all sides. Place in a covered bowl or in a paper bag to rest for 10 to 15 minutes. Peel off the charred skin and discard. Remove the core, stem, and seeds. Purée with the Champagne in a blender or food processor. Can be made in advance and set aside in a covered container.

When scallop pastries go into the oven, place red pepper purée in a saucepan and simmer for 5 minutes. Add sour cream and simmer 5 minutes more. (Do not boil.) Divide the hot pepper sauce among 6 pre-warmed luncheon plates. Top each with a baked scallop pastry.   Serves 6.

Serve with a Champagne (Brut).

Poached Scallops with Tomato Concassée

6 Roma tomatoes
1 tablespoon balsamic vinegar
Salt and pepper
2 cloves garlic, minced
1 cup clam juice

½ cup white wine
1 tablespoon lemon juice
1 teaspoon peppercorns
1 pound scallops

Bring a medium pot of water to a boil. Have ready a bowl of ice water. Drop Roma tomatoes into boiling water for 1 minute then transfer immediately to ice water. This will shock the skin and make it easy to peel. Discard ice water. Using a small knife remove the skin from the tomatoes and slice the long way in half and remove the seeds. To make the concassée, dice tomato into tiny pieces and combine with vinegar, salt, pepper, and garlic. Set aside.

In a 10-inch skillet simmer clam juice with wine, lemon juice and peppercorns. Add scallops and cover, cooking for 5 minutes.

Heat the tomato concassée gently before serving. Remove scallops from poaching broth. Spoon concassée mixture onto individual plates and top with poached scallops. Garnish with chopped parsley and serve.   Serves 4

A dry white wine goes well with this.

Scallops in Onion Cups

2 medium white onions
4 saffron threads
2 cups white wine
2 shallots, thinly sliced
1 medium leek, thinly sliced
1 medium red onion, chopped
½ cup diced chives
4 large scallops

½ cube plus 2 tablespoons
  butter
2 cloves garlic, crushed
1 red bell pepper, seeded,
  roasted and cut in strips
Asiago cheese
Balsamic vinegar
4 Roma tomatoes, diced fine

Cut the white onions in half and trim a small amount off the bottom of the onion so that it is flat and sits straight. Push out the center of the onion. This should give you a single-layer onion cup.

Quickly roast the saffron in a hot, dry pan. In a bowl, mix the roasted saffron with the wine. Set aside and let marinate for 30 minutes.

Heat the wine-saffron mixture in a saucepan. Add the onion cups and cook until al dente. Remove and place in a pan of cold water to stop cooking process. Dry and set aside.

Place the shallots, leek, red onion and ¼ cup chives in the wine and cook until al dente. Remove the red onion mixture with a slotted spoon, cover and set aside. Reduce the remaining liquid down to ¼ cup.

In a sauté pan, sear the scallops with 2 tablespoons of the butter and the garlic. Set aside.

Melt the ½ cube butter on low heat. Add the red onion mixture and the reduced liquid to the melted butter and blend.

To serve, place the onion cup in the middle of a plate and fill with red onion mixture. Place the roasted red bell pepper strips on top of onion mixture and place a scallop on the peppers. Shave asiago cheese over top. Lightly drizzle balsamic vinegar around plate and garnish with the remaining chives and Roma tomatoes.   Serves 4.

Serve with a rich, crisp Chardonnay.

Confetti Mussels

2 cups Sauvignon Blanc wine
2 cloves garlic, finely chopped
½ cup chopped shallots
8 sprigs Italian parsley
1 bay leaf
4 sprigs fresh thyme, or ½
  teaspoon dried

6 quarts mussels, scrubbed
  and soaked in cold water
Vinaigrette (recipe follows)
1 red bell pepper, diced, for
  garnish
1 yellow bell pepper, diced, for
  garnish

Combine first 6 ingredients in a large non-corrosive pot with a tight lid and bring to a boil.

Add mussels, cover and cook over high heat for about 5 minutes. Shake pot up and down several times during cooking to reposition mussels. As soon as mussels open, remove them from the pot. Discard any that have not opened after 8 to 10 minutes in the pot.

Remove mussels from their shells and set aside. Strain cooking liquid and reserve for another use.

VINAIGRETTE:
2 tablespoons finely minced
  shallots
1 tablespoon Sauvignon Blanc
  wine
1 tablespoon lemon juice

Salt and freshly ground black
  pepper
4 tablespoons olive oil

In a large bowl, whisk together shallots, wine and lemon juice. Season with salt and pepper to taste, then whisk in oil.

Toss mussels in vinaigrette and marinate for ½ hour before serving. Arrange each mussel in a half shell on a serving plate. Garnish with red and yellow bell peppers.   Serves 8.

Serve with a Sauvignon Blanc.

Seafood Medley with Lemon, Wine and Cream Sauce

A simple but elegant dish with delicate seafood and a zesty lemon cream sauce.

1 tablespoon butter (softened)
2 tablespoons flour
1 cup water
4 bay or sea scallops
16 prawns, shelled and
 deveined
2 tablespoons chopped
 shallots
1 tablespoon olive oil
1 cup Chardonnay wine
3 tablespoons fresh lemon
 juice

4 tablespoons whipping cream
Salt and pepper
1 package (8 ounces) egg
 noodles, cooked

GARNISH:
Zest of one lemon
1 tablespoon fresh black
 pepper
2 green onions, thinly sliced

Cream together butter and flour, and set aside. In a medium saucepan, salt the cup of water and bring to boil. Poach the scallops 1 minute and add prawns; poach for 1 minute more. Remove seafood and reserve poaching liquid.

Sauté shallots in olive oil, add wine and reduce liquid by half. Add poaching liquid and lemon juice; bring to boil. Add butter/flour mixture a little at a time and whisk until smooth. Lightly simmer sauce for 2 minutes, add cream and salt and pepper to taste.

Serve scallops and shrimp over pasta with lemon cream sauce. Garnish with lemon zest, cracked black pepper and sliced green onions.   Serves 4 as an entrée.

Serve with a Chardonnay or a dry Chenin Blanc.

Fillet of Salmon with a Wine Sauce

2 cups Cabernet Sauvignon
 wine
3 tablespoons balsamic
 vinegar
1 shallot, chopped
1 clove garlic, minced
1 tomato, chopped

1 cup chicken stock
3 tablespoons butter, cut into
 ½-inch pieces
1 ½ pounds salmon fillet, cut
 in 4 pieces, brushed with
 olive oil and seasoned with
 salt and pepper

In a saucepan, combine wine, vinegar, shallot, garlic and tomato. Reduce over medium heat to half the amount. Add chicken stock and reduce by half again. Whisk in the butter.

Heat a non-stick sauté pan over high heat. Add salmon and sear until nicely browned. Finish cooking on reverse side over medium heat. To serve, place on plates and pour warm wine sauce over the salmon.   Serves 4.

Serve with a Cabernet Sauvignon or a Cabernet Franc.

Sautéed Tuna with Vermouth Dill Sauce

2 tablespoons chopped
 shallots
8 tablespoons unsalted butter
1 cup Dry Vermouth
1 tablespoon fresh dill

1 cup clam broth
¼ cup heavy whipping cream
Salt and pepper
2 pounds tuna, sliced in thin
 fillets

To make the Vermouth Dill sauce, sauté shallots in 1 tablespoon of the butter. Add Vermouth and dill; reduce to 1 tablespoon. Add clam broth and reduce again to 2 tablespoons. Add cream and bring to a boil. Whisk in 5 tablespoons of the butter. Salt and pepper to taste. Keep warm.

Sauté the tuna in the remaining 2 tablespoons butter for 3 minutes on each side. To serve, divide tuna among six plates. Garnish with the sauce.   Serves 6.

Serve with a Chardonnay or a Merlot.

Poultry

COOKING WITH WINE

Walnut Crusted Lavender Chicken

8 ounces low-fat plain yogurt
Juice of ½ lemon or lime
¼ cup Sauvignon Blanc wine
1 ½ tablespoons Lavender
  Spice Mix (recipe follows)
1 teaspoon minced fresh garlic

6 chicken breast halves,
  boneless and skinless
½ cup bread crumbs
¼ cup ground walnuts
2 tablespoons flour
Oil and butter for cooking

First, blend all Lavender Spice Mix ingredients.

LAVENDER SPICE MIX:
2 tablespoons salt-free spicy
  pepper seasoning
2 healthy pinches of salt
2 pinches super fine sugar

⅛ teaspoon ground lavender
  buds and flowers
⅛ teaspoon toasted ground
  cumin

Mix ingredients until well blended.

In stainless bowl or glass dish, combine yogurt, lemon or lime juice, wine, Lavender Spice Mix and garlic. Cut chicken breasts into 2 or 3 pieces (cutting across the grain). Pieces should be about 2 ½ to 3 inches in diameter. Pound slightly to make pieces approximately ⅓ × ½ -inch thick. Add to yogurt mixture, cover and refrigerate 1 to 4 hours.

Mix bread crumbs, walnuts and flour in shallow dish. Remove chicken and wipe off some of the yogurt mixture. Dip chicken into bread crumb and walnut mixture coating thoroughly. Heat heavy sauté pan to medium and add about 2 tablespoons each oil and butter. Cook 3 to 4 pieces of chicken at a time allowing plenty of room. Cook chicken 3 to 4 minutes on each side until golden brown and cooked thoroughly. Keep adding oil and butter as necessary. Serve with rice.   Serves 6.

Delicious with a Sauvignon Blanc.

Sautéed Chicken Breasts with
Mushroom Brandy Sauce

6 chicken breasts, boneless
 and skinless
Flour
Salt and pepper
2 tablespoons butter
2 tablespoons olive oil
¼ cup Brandy

2 shallots, minced
1 clove garlic, minced
½ cup sliced shiitake
 mushrooms
1 cup chicken stock
½ cup heavy cream

Lightly pound chicken breasts with mallet and dredge in flour. Season with salt and pepper. In a sauté pan melt the butter and oil together. Sauté chicken until golden brown. Transfer to an oven-proof dish.

Deglaze pan with Brandy and add shallots, garlic and mushrooms. Whisk in chicken stock and cream. Bring to a boil; reduce by half. Place chicken in a 350 degree oven for 10 minutes. Keep sauce warm. Serve chicken with Mushroom Brandy Sauce.   Serves 6.

Serve with a Chardonnay or Fumé Blanc.

Herb Stuffed Chicken

1 bunch fresh sage (at least
 20 leaves)
1 bunch fresh oregano
1 bunch fresh rosemary

1 large roasting chicken
½ cup cream Sherry
Seasoned salt
Curry powder

Stuff the chicken's cavity with the fresh herbs and place it in a roasting pan with a cover. Pour the cream Sherry over the chicken, dust it with seasoned salt and curry powder.

Cover and roast at 350 degrees for approximately one hour, or until brown and tender.   Serves 4 to 6.

Serve this with a dry Gewürztraminer or a spicy red Zinfandel.

Chardonnay Chicken with Grapes on Minted Rice

2 tablespoons minced fresh
  ginger
2 cloves garlic, minced
1 small onion, thinly sliced
1 ½ teaspoons ground cumin
½ teaspoon ground coriander
1 teaspoon salt
½ teaspoon powdered
  mustard
½ teaspoon freshly ground
  black pepper

1 cup Chardonnay wine
1 ¼ pounds chicken breasts,
  skinned and boned
1 tablespoon olive oil
½ pound red or green
  seedless grapes
1 tablespoon butter, cold
Mint sprigs
Minted White and Wild Rice
  (recipe follows)

In a medium bowl, mix fresh ginger, garlic, onion, cumin, coriander, salt, mustard and pepper into wine. Place chicken in bowl and marinate 30 minutes. Remove chicken. Reserve marinade.

Cut chicken breasts into ¾-inch wide strips. Pat dry with paper towel. In non-stick sauté pan, heat olive oil. Brown chicken on both sides. Add marinade and grapes.

Cook over high heat for 5 minutes until chicken is done. Whisk in cold butter until sauce thickens slightly. Meanwhile, prepare Minted White and Wild Rice.

MINTED WHITE AND WILD RICE:
1 cup water
1 cup homemade or low-
  sodium chicken broth
⅛ teaspoon black pepper

¾ cup white and wild rice
  blend
1 ½ tablespoons finely
  chopped fresh mint

In medium saucepan, bring water, broth and pepper to a boil. Add rice. Cover pot and cook over moderate heat for 25 to 30 minutes until water is absorbed and rice is tender. Add freshly chopped mint. Mix well. Serve chicken over ½ cup rice per person. Garnish with fresh mint sprigs.   Makes 6 servings.

Serve with a Chardonnay.

Roasted Range Chicken in Natural Jus

2 tablespoons olive oil
¾ cup medium diced onions
2 tablespoons thinly sliced
 garlic
½ cup medium diced carrots
½ cup medium diced celery

1 fresh range chicken (4
 pounds) rubbed with a
 mixture of fresh sage,
 rosemary and garlic
½ cup Pinot Noir wine
2 bay leaves

Place olive oil in a sauté pan with the onions, garlic, carrots and celery. Sauté over moderate heat until onions are clear. Transfer to a roasting pan.

After rubbing the chicken with fresh sage, rosemary and garlic, sear the bird on all sides in a large sauté pan over high heat. Place into the roasting pan with the sautéed vegetables.

Into a sauté pan, pour ⅓ cup water, the wine and bay leaves. Bring to boil. Pour over chicken and place in a preheated 350 degree oven for 1 hour or until the juices run clear from the chicken when pricking the leg with a fork. Remove the bird from oven and let stand for 15 minutes. Remove bay leaves.

Bone the chicken. Pour the pan juices over chicken before serving. Serve with mixed spring vegetables and French butter beans.

Serves 4.

Serve with a Pinot Noir.

Poultry

Cherry Glazed Cornish Game Hen
with Wild Rice Stuffing,
Snow Peas and Baby Beets

4 Cornish game hens
Salt and black pepper
1 cup wild rice
3 cups chicken stock
½ cup chopped walnuts
3 green onions, chopped
2 cups Pinot Noir wine
1 cup cherry preserves
1 teaspoon cinnamon

3 bunches baby beets
 (approximately 12)
1 cup virgin olive oil
4 tablespoons balsamic
 vinegar
1 can jumbo black olives
1 pound snow peas
¼ pound salad greens

Generously salt and pepper cavity of the game hens. Gently steam for 30 minutes over boiling water; set aside. Cool before stuffing.

Bring wild rice and chicken stock to boil; lower heat and simmer 40 to 45 minutes until chicken stock is absorbed. When slightly cooled add walnuts and green onions. Season with salt and fresh ground black pepper. Stuff each game hen with wild rice mixture. Place on baking sheet.

To prepare the glaze, reduce the wine to ½ cup. Add cherry preserves and reduce until thickened. Add cinnamon and mix well. Brush game hen with cherry glaze place in 400 degree oven. Cook 10 minutes until glaze is bubbling and game hens are tender.

Cook beets until tender; remove skin. Whisk olive oil and vinegar together. Season with salt and freshly ground black pepper. Toss beets and olives in vinaigrette. Blanch snow peas for 16 seconds.

For presentation, fan out snow peas on each side of the plate (to resemble feathers of the hen). Place game hen in center (legs forward). Place a few beets and olives in front of plate (to resemble bird eggs). Make a small bouquet with salad greens and push in between the legs into the rice mixture. Drizzle greens with the vinaigrette dressing.   Serves 4.

Serve with a Pinot Noir.

Sunday Afternoon Chicken Breasts

4 large boneless chicken
  breasts
½ teaspoon salt (optional)
1 tablespoon rosemary,
  crumbled (chopped if fresh)
2 tablespoons olive oil
2 tablespoons fresh lemon
  juice

1 cup Champagne (Brut)
½ teaspoon grated lemon zest
½ teaspoon thyme
½ teaspoon freshly ground
  black pepper
1 tablespoon minced onion
¼ teaspoon paprika

Place chicken breasts in a roasting or baking pan large enough to lay them flat. Sprinkle meat evenly with salt on both sides. In a small bowl, whisk together remaining ingredients, and pour over meat. Cover and refrigerate at least 2 hours or overnight, turning once or twice.

Grill chicken breasts over a medium-hot barbecue fire until firm and no longer pink in the center.

This is a nice summer dish with a spicy potato salad.   Serves 4.

Serve with a Champagne (Brut).

Chicken & Lemon Herb Dumplings with Leek Cream

4 chicken legs
2 tablespoons olive oil
2 bunches leeks, washed and
  cut into ½-inch dice (up to the
  light green)
1 white onion, thinly sliced
1 cup Chardonnay wine
2 cups rich chicken stock
1 sprig of tarragon

½ cup cream
1 tablespoon chopped
  tarragon leaves
¼ pound oyster mushrooms,
  trimmed and brushed
¼ pound pearl onions, tossed
  in oil, roasted and peeled
Dumplings (recipe follows)

Season the chicken legs with salt and pepper. In a skillet, lightly brown the chicken in the olive oil; remove chicken and set aside. In the same skillet, add the leeks and white onion. Cover and sweat over medium heat; do not brown. Add the wine and reduce to 2 tablespoons. Return the chicken to the skillet. Add the chicken stock, and tarragon sprig. Cover and braise until meat is very tender. Remove chicken and de-grease pan.

Blend the leek mixture in a blender. Strain and return to the skillet, then add cream. Remove chicken meat from the bones. Add to leek mixture along with the tarragon, mushrooms and pearl onions. Heat through. Prepare the Dumplings.

DUMPLINGS:
1 pound cake flour
1 ounce sugar
2 tablespoons baking powder
½ teaspoon salt
4 ounces butter
1 cup cream

1 cup sour cream
2 tablespoon lemon zest
1 teaspoon lemon juice
2 tablespoons minced lemon
  thyme

Mix dry ingredients; cut in butter. Add remaining ingredients until it just comes together, then finish by hand. Chill. On a parchment-lined sheet pan, drop 2 tablespoons per dumpling. Brush with cream; bake at 350 degrees for 12 to 18 minutes or golden.

Serve in a casserole with dumplings on top.   Serves 4.

Serve with a Chardonnay.

Chicken Cacciatore #1

6 boneless, skinless chicken
  thighs
⅓ cup olive oil
1 large onion, sliced
3 cloves garlic, chopped
2 to 3 carrots, peeled and
  chopped
¼ cup finely chopped parsley

1 bay leaf
1 can (28 ounces) whole
  Italian tomatoes
1 can (8 ounces) tomato
  sauce
Salt
Freshly ground pepper
½ cup Petite Syrah wine

Rinse chicken and pat dry with paper towels. Heat oil in heavy skillet. Brown chicken well. Remove chicken and add onion, garlic, carrots, and parsley. Sauté over medium heat for about 5 minutes. Add bay leaf, tomatoes and tomato sauce, mixing well. Add chicken, salt, pepper, and wine. Simmer for about 45 minutes over low heat (uncovered for the first 30 minutes, covered for the last 15 minutes). Remove bay leaf.

Serve with polenta, rice or pasta, and, of course, a bottle or two of a Petite Syrah.   Serves 4 to 6.

Chicken Cacciatore #2

1 large yellow onion
Olive oil
2 each fresh chicken legs, thighs and breasts
All purpose flour
Salt and white pepper
1 fresh lemon (cut ½ into rings, juice the other half)
½ cup Chardonnay wine
½ teaspoon Angostura Bitters
⅓ cup of water

Several sprigs fresh marjoram and thyme (or 1 teaspoon each dried marjoram and thyme)
4 to 6 large whole garlic cloves
1 tablespoon capers and juice
Salt and pepper
Freshly grated Romano or Parmesan cheese

Cut onion into rings and sauté in olive oil until limp and golden; set aside.

Season flour with salt and white pepper. Dredge chicken in flour. Sauté chicken over medium heat until golden. Place lemon rings on top of chicken then add onion rings. Add the remaining ingredients, jostle to mix, cover and simmer over low heat for 30 to 35 minutes. Adjust seasoning with salt and pepper to taste.

Sprinkle with freshly grated Romano or Parmesan cheese. Good with rice or risotto and fresh steamed green beans with slivered almonds.   Serves 4 to 6.

Serve with a Chardonnay.

Chicken Breast Dijonaise

1 tablespoon butter	1 clove garlic, minced
1 tablespoon olive oil	¼ cup Chardonnay wine
Flour for dredging	2 tablespoons Dijon mustard
2 boneless chicken breasts	¼ cup heavy whipping cream
Dried basil, thyme and	
oregano	

Preheat oven to 400 degrees. Heat butter and olive oil on the stove top in an oven-proof skillet over medium heat until it sizzles.

Dredge chicken lightly in flour, shaking off the excess. Add chicken to the skillet, skin side down, and brown on both sides. Drain any remaining butter from the pan and sprinkle the chicken lightly with the dried herbs and garlic.

Add the wine and mustard to the skillet and stir to combine. Place skillet into the oven for 20 to 30 minutes, until chicken feels firm to the touch.

Remove skillet and place on stove top. Remove chicken to plates and keep warm. Add cream to the skillet and cook over medium-high heat until sauce thickens and coats the back of a spoon. Pour over chicken and serve immediately.   Serves 2.

Serve with a Chardonnay.

Mustard Roast Chicken with Sage

1 chicken (2 ½ to 3 pounds)
12 fresh sage leaves, washed
 and dried
¾ cup Dijon mustard
2 teaspoons minced sage

2 teaspoons minced parsley
Sea salt and ground pepper
½ cup low-fat sour cream
½ cup chicken stock
½ cup white wine

Remove any visible fat around the tail opening of the bird. Starting from the neck end, use your fingers (do not cut anything) to gently create a space between the skin and the breast meat, and down into each drumstick. Place the sage leaves about 1 inch apart in the space under the skin, to make a random "dotted" pattern. Cover the outside with a thick layer of mustard and sprinkle with one teaspoon of the herbs. Add salt and pepper.

Roast in a preheated 425 degree oven for 20 minutes, then reduce heat to 350 degrees and cook for another 30 minutes. Do not baste. Take chicken from oven and gently smooth on the sour cream. Return to oven and bake 10 minutes more.

When the chicken is cooked, remove to a platter. Pour off any oil or fat in the pan, without removing the brown glaze. Warm the pan over low heat while adding the stock and wine, stirring and gently scraping to incorporate the brown glaze into the sauce. Add the remaining herb mixture, and simmer until reduced by a third.

Cut the chicken into portions, pour an equal amount of the sauce over each.   Serves 4.

Serve with a Chardonnay or Fumé Blanc.

Chicken, Artichoke Hearts & Eggplant

4 tablespoons virgin olive oil
3 skinless, boneless chicken breasts, cut into bite-size pieces
1 medium onion, cut lengthwise into 8 wedges
2 small young oriental eggplants, diced into ¾-inch cubes

1 small jar artichoke hearts (if hearts are large, split in half lengthwise)
½ cup Chardonnay wine
½ to 1 teaspoon Dijon mustard

Heat oil in large skillet, add chicken and sauté for 6 to 8 minutes. Add onion and eggplant. Sauté 3 to 5 minutes stirring occasionally. Stir in artichoke hearts and cook for 1 more minute.

Add wine and Dijon mustard. Cook for 5 minutes to thoroughly mix and heat ingredients. Serve over rice or noodles.

This is a great quick supper idea. All you need to make it perfect is a glass of the same Chardonnay you used in the sauce.

Serves 2.

Chicken in Shallot Cream Sauce

4 half breasts of chicken,
  skinned and boned
½ cup flour mixed with salt,
  pepper and dried sage to
  taste
4 tablespoons butter

2 shallots, finely diced
½ cup Chardonnay wine
¼ cup heavy cream
1 to 2 tablespoons chopped
  fresh parsley for garnish

Lightly flour each chicken breast with the flour/spice mixture. Set aside while melting butter over medium heat in a sauté pan. Add chicken to pan and cook 5 to 6 minutes per side, until lightly browned. Transfer chicken to warm oven. Pour off excess fat from sauté pan and quickly sauté shallots until soft and slightly golden. Increase heat and pour in wine. Reduce the wine to ¼ cup, scraping bottom of pan as it reduces. Lower heat and stir in cream.

When warm throughout, pour sauce into a wire strainer and press as much liquid from the shallots as possible. Discard shallots and return sauce to pan. Add chopped parsley and additional salt and pepper if needed. Heat gently.

To serve, pour a small amount of the sauce on each plate, top with a chicken breast and cover chicken with additional sauce. Garnish with fresh parsley or fresh sage.   Serves 4.

Serve with a Chardonnay.

Country Style Chicken

An old family recipe, this chicken dish is easy to make and filled with lots of big, hearty, rustic flavors of tomatoes, onions and the rich, earthy flavors of Cabernet Sauvignon.

2 tablespoons olive oil
1 ½ pounds boneless, skinless
  chicken thighs or breasts
1 medium onion, chopped
¾ cup Cabernet Sauvignon
  wine
2 carrots, cut in 1 inch rounds
1 can (28 ounces) diced
  tomatoes, with juice

6 cloves garlic, peeled, cut in
  half
1 can (15 ¾ ounces) garbanzo
  beans, drained
1 lemon, cut into 8 pieces
4 tablespoons capers
½ teaspoon crushed red
  pepper flakes
Salt and pepper

In heavy medium saucepan, heat oil and brown chicken. Add onions and sauté 2 more minutes. Add wine and reduce liquid for about 5 minutes. Add carrots, tomatoes with their juice, garlic, garbanzo beans, lemon, capers and pepper flakes. Cook on medium heat for 15 minutes. Remove lemon pieces. Salt and pepper to taste. Cook another 15 minutes.

Serve with boiled potatoes, rice or pasta.   Serves 6.

Serve with a Cabernet Sauvignon.

Chicken Primavera

Fresh herbs must be used for this recipe. If you cannot find those listed, substitute with other comparable fresh herbs.

¼ ounce dried porcini mushrooms (equivalent of about 2 medium mushrooms)
30 fresh sage leaves, 1 inch long
3 tablespoons olive oil
3 medium cloves garlic, chopped
½ teaspoon salt
⅛ teaspoon fine black pepper
4 large boneless chicken breast halves (5 to 6 ounces each)
½ cup Chardonnay wine
1 tablespoon chopped fresh chives or spring green onions
1 tablespoon chopped Italian parsley

Soak porcini mushrooms in ½ cup hot water for at least 30 minutes (save soaking liquid). Rinse mushrooms to remove any loose dirt. Strain reserved mushroom liquid into a blender using a fine mesh strainer (or a larger mesh lined with a paper towel). Add porcini and blend on high speed until mushrooms become a thick liquid. Set aside. (This makes about ½ cup of porcini purée. Since only 2 tablespoons are used for this recipe, reserve remainder for use as a flavoring in soups, red sauces, or simply toss with hot pasta!)

Chop about 10 leaves of sage to make one heaping tablespoon. Mix with oil, garlic, salt and pepper. Coat chicken breasts with this oil mixture and sauté over medium-high heat for 4 minutes. Turn heat to medium-low and sauté the second side for 6 to 8 minutes. Cut a slit in breast and check for doneness. Meat should not be pink. Remove chicken to warm serving platter.

Over medium-high heat, add wine to skillet, stirring to incorporate browned bits on the bottom. Reduce slightly for several minutes. Then add 2 tablespoons of porcini purée. Reduce for another minute and add remaining sage leaves, chives and parsley. Leave over flame just long enough to heat greens and retain their bright color. When sauce is hot, pour over chicken breasts and serve immediately.   Serves 4.

The chicken and herb flavors are a natural match with Chardonnay.

Brandied Chicken

1 pound sliced fresh
  mushrooms
4 tablespoons butter
6 large chicken breasts
½ teaspoon salt
½ teaspoon pepper
¼ cup Brandy

1 teaspoon thyme
1 cup dry white wine
2 tablespoons cornstarch
⅓ cup water
½ cup chopped green onions,
  stems and tops

Sauté mushrooms in butter in a large skillet. Remove mushrooms and reserve. Brown chicken well. Sprinkle with salt and pepper during browning. Add Brandy, pouring over chicken. Sprinkle thyme over chicken. Remove from heat. Add wine, cover and simmer 35 minutes until chicken is tender.

Remove chicken to a heated serving platter. Skim excess fat from pan juices, if any. Stir cornstarch into water; add to pan juices and heat, stirring constantly, until mixture thickens and boils. Stir in reserved mushrooms and green onions. Cook one minute. Spoon over chicken. Serve at once with rice or egg noodles.   Serves 6.

Serve with a Chardonnay or Fumé Blanc.

Rosemary Roast Chicken

The sweet perfume of the rosemary adds a lovely nuance to the chicken.

1 whole chicken (3 to 5 pounds)	Potatoes (two per person)
1 tablespoon olive oil	Fresh long green beans (½ pound per person)
4 cloves garlic, peeled and minced	¼ cup butter
½ cup chopped fresh rosemary leaves	A small amount of cream or milk
Salt and pepper	1 to 2 cups Chenin Blanc wine

Preheat oven to 400 degrees. Place the chicken in a large roasting pan, legs up, and lightly drizzle the olive oil all over it. Mince two cloves of the garlic and rub into the skin of the chicken. Chop the rosemary leaves coarsely and sprinkle them over the entire chicken, evenly coating it with a fine layer. Add salt and pepper to taste. Lower oven to 350 degrees and roast the chicken for one hour or so, until fork tender (fork should penetrate meat easily).

While chicken roasts, peel the potatoes and cover with salted water in a heavy pot. Add the remaining 2 cloves of garlic and boil with the potatoes until potatoes are just tender, but not falling apart. Remove from heat, drain well. Add butter and a little cream or milk. Mash potatoes and garlic into a smooth purée. Salt and pepper to taste. Clean the beans. Place in a steamer (or cover in water and boil). Steam until tender; drain well.

About 10 minutes before the chicken is done, remove from oven, drizzle wine over it, and put it back in the oven to finish cooking. The wine will deglaze the pan and you can use this remaining juice as a sauce to spoon over the chicken. Serve with the garlic mashed potatoes and steamed green beans. Serves 4 to 6.

Serve with a Chenin Blanc.

Chicken Monterey Jack

6 boneless chicken breasts	1 cup Chardonnay wine
2 tablespoons olive oil	3 ripe avocados, mashed
2 cups sliced button mushrooms	1 cup grated Monterey jack cheese
2 to 3 cloves garlic, chopped	

Sauté chicken in olive oil until just done. Remove to oven-proof dish.

Sauté mushrooms and garlic in same pan adding more olive oil if necessary. Deglaze pan with the wine and reduce to about ⅓ cup.

Add mashed avocados to make a very thick sauce. It should be the consistency of guacamole. Thin with more wine if necessary and season with salt and pepper if desired.

Spoon sauce over chicken in baking dish. Top with cheese and bake in a 350 degree oven until cheese is melted and dish is heated through. Serve with rice. Serves 4 to 6 people.

Enjoy with a Chardonnay.

Indonesian Chicken Breasts

6 skinless boneless chicken
  breasts

MARINADE:
4 tablespoons Sauvignon
  Blanc wine, or 3 tablespoons
  dry white wine and 1
  tablespoon honey
4 cloves garlic, finely minced
2 tablespoons hoisin sauce
1 tablespoon minced fresh
  cilantro

1 tablespoon finely minced
  ginger
1 green onion, minced
1 shallot, minced
1 tablespoon distilled white
  vinegar
2 tablespoons soy sauce
1 tablespoon sesame oil
1 tablespoon plum sauce
1 tablespoon peanut butter
1 teaspoon Chinese chili paste
  with garlic

Gently flatten chicken breasts to uniform thickness.

Combine marinade ingredients. Divide marinade in half and store
half in refrigerator for use as a dipping sauce. Use the other half to
marinate the chicken in the refrigerator from 1 to 8 hours.

About an hour before cooking, light coals (preferably mesquite) in
a kettle-type barbecue. If desired, sprinkle hickory chips that have
been soaked in water for 10 minutes over the hot coals.

Place marinated chicken on the grill and cover kettle so chicken
smokes as it cooks. Cook chicken breasts until done, about 5
minutes on each side. Serve the reserved marinade as dipping
sauce.   Serves 4 to 6.

Serve with a Sauvignon Blanc.

A Special Chicken Scallopine

3 whole skinless and boneless
  chicken breasts
⅓ cup plus 1 to 2 tablespoons
  flour
Pure or light olive oil
1 large onion, chopped

1 pound cremini or button
  mushrooms, quartered
4 to 5 garlic cloves, sliced
1 ½ cups low-sodium chicken
  broth
1 cup Chardonnay wine

Slice chicken into 1½-inch strips and dredge in ⅓ cup flour seasoned with salt and pepper. Brown the strips in olive oil in a skillet. Remove the chicken and add a bit more olive oil to the skillet. Sauté onion until soft; add mushrooms and garlic.

Continue sautéing until mushrooms are soft and have given up their liquid. Add broth, wine and chicken. Cover and cook for another 15 to 20 minutes on low heat. Add remaining 1 to 2 tablespoons flour to thicken sauce. Serve over rice.   Serves 4.

Enjoy with a glass of Chardonnay.

Mushroom Chicken

8 boneless, skinless chicken breasts	¾ cup butter
½ cup flour	¾ pound mushrooms, thinly sliced
1 teaspoon season salt	1 cup heavy cream
1 teaspoon ground pepper	⅓ cup Champagne (Brut)

Place chicken breasts between wax paper and pound until flattened, approximately ¼-inch thick. Lightly coat with flour, season with salt and ground pepper (dredge and shake off excess).

Melt butter in non-stick skillet and cook breasts until lightly brown on each side -- do not overcook. Add the mushrooms and sauté for approximately 10 to 12 minutes. Pour off and reserve any excess butter* for other use.

Add heavy cream and simmer. Stir frequently for approximately 10 minutes. Place only the breasts in a covered casserole and place in warm oven.

Add Champagne to the mixture, and bring to a rolling boil and reduce sauce to a creamy consistency. If sauce is too thick, add more Champagne. Place breasts on large serving platter and spoon mushroom cream sauce over top. The delicate flavors of the sautéed chicken and the fresh bright flavors of the Champagne will make this dish a favorite. Serves 6 to 8.

*If desired, sauté a number of large mushroom caps for garnish in the reserved butter.

Serve with a Champagne (Brut).

Chicken Breasts with Stilton Cheese and Leeks

5 tablespoons minced shallots
4 tablespoons butter
6 chicken breasts, skinned and
  boned
1 cup Sauvignon Blanc wine
2 ½ cups whipping cream

2 ounces Stilton cheese
Pinch cayenne pepper
4 medium leeks, washed and
  sliced (including part of
  green)
Salt and pepper

Sauté 3 tablespoons of the shallots in 2 tablespoons of the butter for several minutes. Add chicken and cook gently on both sides without browning. Add wine, bring to a boil and add the cream. Simmer the chicken for 6 or 7 minutes or until tender. Remove the chicken and keep warm. Add cheese to sauce and stir until melted. Add cayenne.

In another pan sauté leeks with the remaining shallots in the remaining 2 tablespoons of butter until just tender. Add salt and pepper to taste. Divide leeks among six plates. Place a chicken breast on top and then strain the sauce over chicken.

Diced red peppers sautéed with the leeks are a pretty addition. Serve with mixed wild and long grain rice.   Serves 6.

Serve with a Sauvignon Blanc.

Sauvignon Blanc Poached Chicken

4 chicken breasts
1 tablespoon olive or canola oil
2 garlic cloves, crushed and
  chopped

2 cups Sauvignon Blanc wine
6 scallions, sliced diagonally
Salt and pepper

Rinse and pat the chicken breasts dry. Heat the oil over medium-high heat in a non-stick skillet. Add the garlic and cook for 1 to 2 minutes, making sure it does not brown or burn. Add the chicken breasts and cook 1 to 2 minutes on each side. Add wine to the skillet, turn up the heat and bring the liquid to a boil, reduce the heat back to medium and cover the skillet. Cook for 5 minutes. Turn over the chicken, add more wine if necessary, cover the skillet and cook for an additional 5 minutes.

Check the chicken to make the sure the temperature is between 150 and 160 degrees. Place the chicken breasts on a warm plate and set aside.

Add the scallions to the poaching liquid and reduce over high heat for approximately 2 minutes until the liquid becomes somewhat syrupy. Return the chicken to the skillet, turning to coat with liquid. Add salt and pepper to taste.   Serves 4.

Serve with a Sauvignon Blanc.

Chicken Gewürztraminer

4 tablespoons butter
2 tablespoons vegetable oil
2 ½ to 3 pounds chicken, cut
 up
1 package frozen small onions
1 teaspoon lemon juice

1 package frozen artichoke
 hearts, defrosted and drained
½ cup Gewürztraminer wine
½ cup chicken stock
Salt and pepper
2 bay leaves

Melt butter and oil in a 10 or 12-inch skillet over medium-high heat and brown chicken pieces. Remove from skillet and place in baking dish. Brown onions until golden. Place in baking dish with chicken.

In the same skillet, add lemon juice and sauté artichoke hearts slightly. Add to the baking dish with chicken and onions. Combine wine, chicken stock, salt, pepper and bay leaves. Pour over chicken baking dish. Bake in a 350 degree oven for 30 minutes or until done. Remove bay leaves before serving.   Serves 4.

Serve with a Gewürztraminer.

Chicken Marinated in White Wine and Dijon Mustard

¾ cup white wine
2 tablespoon cider vinegar
2 tablespoon Dijon mustard
1 tablespoon coarse cracked
 pepper

2 tablespoons minced garlic
¼ cup peanut oil
1 tablespoon rosemary
1 chicken, cut into serving
 pieces

Pour wine and cider vinegar in a saucepan and reduce by half over high heat. Add mustard, pepper, garlic, peanut oil and rosemary. Pour over chicken and marinate for 2 to 8 hours.

When ready to grill, rub marinade off and season with salt. Grill over medium-hot fire.   Serves 4.

Serve with a Chardonnay or Sauvignon Blanc.

Roasted Chicken with Chilies and Herbs

2 tablespoons olive oil
4 tablespoons fresh lime juice
2 jalapeno chilies, seeded and
 finely chopped
1 small onion, minced
1 clove garlic, minced
1 teaspoon finely chopped
 fresh rosemary

1 teaspoon salt
4 boneless chicken breasts
½ cup Chardonnay wine
2 small plum tomatoes,
 chopped
Salt and pepper

Mix olive oil, lime juice, chilies, onion, garlic, rosemary and salt in small bowl. Lift the skin of the chicken breasts and stuff part of this mixture under the skin. Add the remaining mixture to the wine, along with the tomatoes.

Place the chicken in shallow roasting pan and sprinkle with salt and pepper. Pour wine mixture over chicken.

Bake in a 500 degree oven for 5 minutes, lower oven temperature to 350 degrees and bake for an additional 25 minutes, or until chicken is done.   Serves 4.

Serve with a Chardonnay or Sauvignon Blanc.

Chicken Gewürz

18 small pearl onions, peeled
2 stalks celery with leaves,
  minced
3 carrots, finely diced
3 parsnips, finely diced
1 cup button mushrooms (or
  quartered mushrooms)
1 tablespoon olive oil

3 pound fryer, cut into pieces
Salt and pepper
2 cups Gewürztraminer wine
2 cups chicken stock
½ cup Brandy
1 cup cream
¼ cup chopped fresh parsley

Sauté vegetables in the olive oil a stock pot over medium heat, until slightly softened. Lay the chicken pieces on top. Salt and pepper generously, then add the wine and stock to cover. Bring to a boil, then simmer over medium heat until the chicken is tender and cooked through, about 20 minutes. Add the Brandy and cream and cook a few minutes longer. Serve over noodles sprinkled with parsley.   Serves 4.

Serve with a Gewürztraminer.

Turkey Layer-Bake with Spaghetti Squash and Vegetables

1 spaghetti squash, approximately 4 pounds
8 tablespoons olive oil
3 medium zucchini, sliced ¼-inch thick
1 pound button mushrooms, halved
1 large red onion, halved and sliced thin
3 cloves garlic, minced
Flour for dusting

2 pounds turkey breast slices, ⅓-inch thick
¾ cup Merlot wine
1 can (28 ounces) crushed tomatoes
⅓ cup minced fresh basil
½ cup plus 3 tablespoons minced fresh parsley
1 cup grated Parmesan or Romano cheese
2 tablespoons fresh chives

Cut spaghetti squash in half lengthwise; remove seeds. Place both halves cut side down on baking sheet; bake at 350 degrees for 40 minutes. Cool; remove "spaghetti" from squash halves and put into bottom of lightly oiled 13 × 9-inch glass baking dish.

In sauté pan on high heat in 3 tablespoons of the olive oil, sauté the zucchini, mushrooms, and onions for 5 minutes. Add the garlic and cook for 2 minutes more. Remove vegetables from pan and place on top of the spaghetti squash, leaving a center strip open for the turkey. In the same sauté pan, heat 3 tablespoons of the olive oil. Sauté flour-dusted turkey slices for 2 minutes per side. Remove from pan and layer down center of baking dish. Add wine to deglaze the sauté pan, then pour over turkey.

Put same pan back on the heat. Add the remaining 2 tablespoons olive oil, tomatoes, basil, and parsley. Simmer on medium heat for 6 minutes, then drizzle over the vegetables in the baking dish. Sprinkle cheese over the entire dish; cover with foil.

At this point, this one-dish dinner can be refrigerated overnight or cooked at once. When ready to cook, bake, covered, in middle of 350 degree oven for 30 minutes. Then remove foil for 10 minutes. Garnish with parsley and chives. Serve with green salad and French bread.   Serves 6 to 8.

You'll enjoy a Merlot with this one-dish meal.

Breaded Turkey Slices Au Cabernet

Juice of 1 large lemon or ¼
  cup lemon juice concentrate
¼ cup Cabernet Blanc wine
1 small onion, shredded
1 pound turkey slices,
  pounded flat
3 eggs, lightly beaten

1 cup unseasoned bread
  crumbs (spread on wax
  paper)
½ cup flour
Vegetable oil ⅜-inch up the
  side of the skillet.
Salt and pepper

Prepare marinade by mixing together lemon juice, wine and shredded onion.

Pound turkey pieces very thin and place in a bowl with marinade. Add salt and pepper at this time. Leave for at least 2 hours in the marinade.

Roll each turkey slice in flour one at a time and coat well. Dip each slice in the egg mixture. Coat with bread crumbs. As you turn the slices over, place a piece of wax paper over the slice and tap it into the bread crumbs with the palm of your hand to get a better adherence of the crumbs to the meat. (You may prepare them up to this point a few hours ahead of time.)

Heat the oil in a heavy skillet over medium-high heat. Make sure oil is hot enough that it sizzles before you begin. Cook as many slices at one time as will fit loosely in a single layer in the skillet. Remove them just as soon as they are brown and crisp on both sides, which will be very quickly. The meat will be done because it is so thin.

Place the browned meat on paper towels, which will absorb any excess oil. Serve piping hot with lemon wedges and cranberry sauce.   Serves 4 to 6.

Serve with a Cabernet Blanc.

Turkey Meatballs in Caper and Lemon Sauce

3 eggs, lightly beaten
2 tablespoons finely chopped
  green onions
2 tablespoons capers, rinsed
  and minced
1 ¼ pounds ground turkey
½ cup fresh bread crumbs
1 ¼ cups Sauvignon Blanc
  wine
1 cup chicken broth

2 bay leaves
Juice of 1 lemon
Strip of lemon zest, made with
  potato peeler
1 tablespoon cornstarch
Salt and pepper
½ cup sour cream, light if
  desired
1 tablespoon whole capers
Parsley for garnish

Mix eggs, onions, capers, turkey and bread crumbs and form into balls that are 1 inch in diameter.

In a saucepan mix 1 cup of the wine, chicken broth, bay leaves, lemon juice and zest. Bring to a boil and drop turkey meatballs in. Simmer gently for about 15 minutes until meat is cooked. Remove meatballs, lemon zest and bay leaves. Mix cornstarch and the remaining ¼ cup wine, whisk into broth and cook until thickened. Stir in sour cream and whole capers along with meatballs and reheat, being careful not to boil.

Serve on pasta or rice, and garnish with chopped parsley.

Makes 6 servings.

Serve with a Sauvignon Blanc.

Desserts

COOKING WITH WINE

Truffled Fudge Cheesecake
with Raspberry Sauce

3 packages (8 ounces each) cream cheese, softened
1 can (14 ounces) sweetened condensed milk
4 eggs
2 teaspoons vanilla extract

12 ounces semi-sweet chocolate, melted
Raspberry Sauce (recipe follows)
Mint leaves for garnish

Preheat oven to 300 degrees. Prepare Chocolate Crumb Crust.

CHOCOLATE CRUMB CRUST:
1 ½ cups vanilla wafer crumbs
½ cup confectioners sugar

⅓ cup unsweetened cocoa
⅓ cup butter, melted

Combine all ingredients, mixing thoroughly. Press mixture firmly on bottom of 9-inch springform pan. Set aside.

In large mixer bowl, beat cream cheese until fluffy. Gradually beat in milk until smooth. Add eggs, vanilla and melted chocolate and beat well. Pour into prepared crust. Bake for 1 hour and 5 minutes, or until center is set. Cool to room temperature; then chill in the refrigerator.

RASPBERRY SAUCE:
2 ½ tablespoons butter, melted
8 ounces raspberry preserves
3 tablespoons Zinfandel wine

2 tablespoons Brandy
½ cup raspberries, fresh or frozen

Combine ingredients in saucepan. Cook over medium heat for about 10 minutes. Cool.

Serve this delicious cheesecake with Raspberry Sauce, a fresh mint garnish and a glass of Zinfandel.   Serves 8.

Pears and Blackberries In Zinfandel

4 pears
Juice of 1 lemon
3 ½ cups Zinfandel wine
1 vanilla bean
1 teaspoon ground cinnamon

¼ cup sugar
½ pound blackberries, rinsed
Fresh mint leaves for garnish
Powdered sugar and cocoa
 powder for dusting

Peel and core pears from bottom, as to leave the pears whole. Take a small slice off the bottom so that the pears stand upright. Store in cool water with lemon juice so they won't brown. Set aside.

Bring wine, vanilla bean, cinnamon and sugar to a boil in a stainless steel stock pot.

Turn down heat to slow rolling boil; gently lower pears into liquid and poach until just tender, but still firm. Remove and drain pears, saving 1 cup liquid.

In a clean saucepan, add 1 cup of the wine poaching liquid and blackberries. Cook for 1 to 2 minutes, until just warm.   Don't overcook the berries.

Serve by spooning berries and liquid over pears in an upright position. Garnish with mint leaves and dust with powdered sugar and cocoa powder.   Serves 4.

Serve with a Zinfandel.

Hazelnut Tuile

1 ¾ cups ground hazelnuts
3 tablespoons flour
1 ¾ cups sugar

4 egg whites
3 tablespoons butter, melted
Brandy Truffle (recipe follows)

Grind hazelnuts and flour in food processor. In a bowl, combine the ground mixture with the sugar, egg whites and melted butter; mix until smooth.

Line a cookie sheet with parchment paper; butter and flour the parchment. With a small spatula, spread mixture in 3-inch circles. Bake at 300 degrees until golden. While still hot, roll into cigarette or cone shapes on a round wooden spoon handle. Cool Tuiles and store in air tight container. Meanwhile, prepare Brandy Truffle.

BRANDY TRUFFLE:
1 pound chocolate
1 cup heavy cream

3 tablespoons Brandy (to taste)

Chop chocolate and place in a bowl. Bring cream to boil and pour over chocolate. Stir until melted, add Brandy. Cool.

With a piping bag, fill Tuiles with Brandy Truffle. Store leftover Tuiles, if any, in an airtight container in refrigerator for further use.
Serves 4 to 6.

Serve with a Champagne.

Stuffed Baked Pears

4 ripe pears, peeled and cut in half   Vanilla Sauce (recipe follows)
Filling (recipe follows)   Mint springs for garnish

Core and cut a thin slice off the back of each pear half so that it will sit flat on a plate. Rub lemon juice on pears so they won't turn brown.

FILLING:

½ cup plump raisins   2 tablespoons butter
3 tablespoons Brandy   ½ teaspoon freshly grated
¼ cup sugar   nutmeg
2 teaspoons cinnamon

In a food processor, chop the filling ingredients until finely mixed.

Butter a glass baking dish. Stuff pear halves generously and place them close together in the dish. Cover loosely with foil. Bake for ½ hour at 400 degrees. Meanwhile, prepare Vanilla Sauce.

VANILLA SAUCE:

2 cups half-and-half   2 egg yolks
2 teaspoon vanilla   ¼ cup sugar
2 teaspoons Brandy   2 tablespoons cornstarch

In a small pan, heat half-and-half, vanilla, and Brandy. After the mixture is warm, add remaining ingredients. Whisk over low heat until thickened slightly.

Arrange each warm pear half on a pool of Vanilla Sauce and garnish with a mint sprig at the stem end.   Serves 8.

Serve with Champagne.

Cheesecake with Strawberries
Marinated in Champagne

1 ½ pounds cream cheese	Zest of half a lemon
3 ½ eggs	2 pints strawberries, cleaned
¾ cup sugar	and stemmed
1 cup sour cream	½ cup sugar
1 tablespoon vanilla	1 ½ cups Champagne (Brut)

Blend first 6 ingredients and mix with electric mixer for 10 minutes.

Line springform cake pan with aluminum foil, making sure it is water-tight. Pour in the mixture.

Place cake pan in a larger pan, then fill bottom pan with enough water to come half way up on the cake pan. Bake for 45 minutes at 325 degrees.

Remove from the oven and let cool either at room temperature or in the refrigerator.

Marinate 1 pint of the strawberries in the Champagne with ¼ cup of the sugar for 2 hours.

In a saucepan, cook the remaining 1 pint of strawberries with the remaining ¼ cup of the sugar over medium heat for about 10 minutes. Then blend in a blender. Let cool.

Serve the cheesecake garnished with a spoonful of marinated strawberries and a spoonful of strawberry sauce.   Serves 8.

Serve with Champagne (Brut).

Bavarian Cream with Blackberry Sauce

2 teaspoons unflavored gelatin
¾ cup milk
1 egg yolk
2 tablespoons sugar

½ teaspoon vanilla
¾ cup heavy cream, whipped
Blackberry Sauce (recipe
  follows)

Soften gelatin in cold milk, then heat to dissolve. Add egg yolk, sugar and vanilla and cook over medium heat until thickened, stirring constantly. Cool slightly and fold in whipped cream. Divide between eight ⅓-cup molds and refrigerate until set. Meanwhile, prepare Blackberry Sauce.

BLACKBERRY SAUCE:
1 cup blackberries, puréed
  and strained to remove
  seeds
1 tablespoon butter
1 tablespoon lime juice

⅓ cup sugar
¾ cup Sauvignon Blanc wine
¼ cup Crème de Cassis
  liqueur
1 tablespoon cornstarch

In saucepan blend blackberry purée, butter, lime juice, sugar and wine. Blend Creme de Cassis and cornstarch and add to blackberry mixture. Cook over medium heat stirring until sauce thickens. Chill well. Makes two cups. (May be frozen for later use.)

To serve, place a small amount of blackberry sauce in middle of plate and unmold Bavarian Cream in middle. Garnish with mint leaves and additional whole berries.   Serves 8.

Serve with a Sauvignon Blanc.

Zinfandel Cake

2 ¼ cups cake flour, sifted
2 ½ teaspoons baking powder
½ teaspoon cinnamon
½ teaspoon ground cloves
½ teaspoon salt
¼ cup butter
¼ cup vegetable shortening
1 ¼ cups sugar

3 tablespoons orange rind, grated
⅔ cup Zinfandel wine
¼ cup buttermilk
1 tablespoon orange liqueur
½ cup ground walnuts
4 egg whites

Preheat oven to 375 degrees. Grease and flour two 9-inch cake pans. In a bowl, mix together the first 5 ingredients.

In large bowl, cream butter and shortening. Add 1 cup of the sugar and grated orange rind. Cream until fluffy.

Combine Zinfandel, buttermilk and orange liqueur. Add flour mixture, walnuts and Zinfandel mixture to creamed butter mixture and stir until smooth.

Whip egg whites until foamy. Gradually beat in the remaining ¼ cup sugar by the spoonful. Continue beating egg whites until stiff, then fold into cake batter lightly.

Place batter in buttered cake pans. Bake 25 to 30 minutes. Cool and serve with whipped cream or ice cream. Serves 8 generously.

Wine suggestion: Zinfandel, with its blackberry flavor, is especially good with this Zinfandel cake.

171

Spiced Persimmon Pudding

1 cup puréed skinless
  persimmon
2 teaspoons baking powder
1 ½ cups sugar
¼ pound butter
2 eggs
1 tablespoon lemon juice
¼ cup Brandy
1 cup flour

1 teaspoon cinnamon
½ teaspoon allspice
1 teaspoon nutmeg
1 teaspoon grated fresh
  orange peel
½ teaspoon salt
1 cup chopped walnuts
1 cup golden raisins

Combine the persimmon purée with the baking powder in a mixing bowl and set aside.

In another bowl, cream together sugar and butter. Add the eggs, lemon juice and Brandy. Stir in flour, cinnamon, allspice, nutmeg, orange peel and salt. Combine with persimmon mixture. Add walnuts and raisins. Spoon batter into 6 individual greased molds.

Place molds into baking dish. Add enough water to cover molds halfway up the sides. Cover with foil and bake in a 325 degree oven for 2 hours. Serve warm with whipped cream seasoned with Brandy.

Serves 6.

Serve with a dry white wine.

Warm Polenta Cake
with Strawberries Macerated in Zinfandel

¼ cup golden raisins
¼ cup white wine
2 cups ricotta cheese
2 cups Mascarpone cheese
1 cup sugar
1 teaspoon vanilla extract
1 tablespoon crushed fennel
  seed

¾ cup polenta
1 tablespoon butter
Powdered sugar
2 pints strawberries, cleaned
  and sliced
¼ cup sugar
1 cup Zinfandel wine

Preheat oven to 300 degrees. Cover raisins with white wine in a small saucepan. Place on the stove and bring to boil. Remove from the heat and allow to soften for 20 minutes, then drain.

Whisk togther the ricotta, Mascarpone, sugar, vanilla and fennel until smooth. Add the polenta and raisins; stir to combine. Pour into a buttered springform pan. Bake in preheated oven for about 1 hour and 15 minutes, but still liquid in the center.

Remove from oven and allow to cool slightly. Dust with powdered sugar and cut into serving portions.

Toss strawberries with sugar. Adjust quantity of sugar to the sweetness of the berries. Cover with Zinfandel. Allow to stand for 1 hour before serving.

Serve polenta cake over the strawberries.   Serves 10 to 12.

Enjoy with a glass of Zinfandel.

Spiced Brandy Apple Cake

1 ½ cups diced peeled and
  seeded apples
¼ cup Brandy
½ cup flour
¾ cup sugar
2 teaspoons baking powder
1 dash salt
½ teaspoon cinnamon

½ teaspoon nutmeg
¼ teaspoon allspice
1 tablespoon fresh grated
  orange rind
2 teaspoons vanilla
1 egg, beaten
½ cup chopped walnuts
Mint sprigs, for garnish

Marinate apples in Brandy in a mixing bowl and set aside.

Combine flour, sugar, baking powder, salt, cinnamon, nutmeg, allspice and orange rind. Mix thoroughly. Stir in vanilla, egg, apples with Brandy, and walnuts. With a plastic spatula scrape mixture into a greased cake pan.

Bake in a 350 degree oven for 20 minutes. Serve warm with crème anglaise* or whipped cream seasoned with Brandy. Garnish with mint sprigs.   Serves 6.

*Crème anglaise is a rich custard sauce, that can be served hot or cold over cake.

Serve with a Moscato Canelli.

Holiday Brandied Fruit Cake

1 pound butter, melted
2 cups sugar
½ teaspoon salt
Grated zest of 1 lemon
8 eggs
2 cups cake flour
1 tablespoon baking powder
1 cup Champagne (Demi-Sec)

1 cup Brandy
1 ½ cups dried cherries
1 ½ cups walnuts
2 ½ cups pecans
1 ½ cups golden raisins
2 cups glazed pineapple, cut
  into small chunks

Mix together the butter, sugar, salt and lemon zest. Beat the eggs in one at a time. Mix together the flour and baking powder. Slowly add and mix until just incorporated.

In a small pot, heat the Champagne, Brandy and cherries over a medium flame. Cook until the cherries are plumped and most of the liquid has evaporated. When cool, drain the cherries and add to the batter.

Mix well, then fold in walnuts, pecans, raisins and pineapple chunks. Put in greased and floured, paper-lined loaf pans.

Bake for approximately 45 minutes at 350 degrees until the tops are brown and the cake springs back to the touch.

Makes 6 small loaves.

Serve with a Champagne (Demi-Sec).

Walnut Cake

1 egg
5 egg yolks
3 teaspoons Sherry
1 ½ cups powdered sugar
1 ½ cups ground walnuts
1 teaspoon cinnamon

1 teaspoon baking powder
½ cup bread crumbs
5 egg whites
½ pint whipping cream
Dark chocolate bar, flaked

Preheat oven to 300 degrees. Combine whole egg, egg yolks, Sherry and powdered sugar. Beat until creamy and frothy. Combine dry ingredients. Fold into egg mixture.

Whisk 5 egg whites until stiff and fold gently into the yolk mixture. Do not mix, as this is a flourless cake.

Pour into two 8-inch greased and floured cake tins. Bake for 50 minutes at 300 degrees or until done. Carefully remove from the oven. Cool thoroughly.

After cake is completely cool, cover the bottom layer with a generous amount of whipped cream. Top with second layer and frost outside of cake top and sides with whipped cream. Sprinkle chocolate flakes on top.   Serves 6 to 8.

Serve with a chilled Sauvignon Blanc

Kugelhopf

This light cake originated in Austria, and is now a favorite in Germany, France and Poland.

½ cup finely chopped almonds
1 cup raisins
¼ cup Late Harvest Zinfandel*
  wine
½ pound butter
1 ¼ cups sugar

5 eggs
1 teaspoon vanilla
2 ⅓ cups all-purpose flour
2 ½ teaspoons baking powder
¾ teaspoon salt

Butter an 8-inch Kugelhopf fluted ring mold and coat the bottom and sides with finely chopped almonds.

Soak the raisins in the wine. Cream butter, add sugar and beat until smooth. Beat in eggs and vanilla.

Sift flour, baking powder and salt together in a bowl. Gradually add to the egg mixture and mix just until smooth. Do not over beat. Stir in raisins and wine and mix until combined.

Pour batter into prepared cake pan. Bake in a preheated 350 degree oven for 35 to 45 minutes, until a toothpick inserted in center of the cake comes out clean.

Let cake settle in pan for 10 to 15 minutes and turn out on a plate while still warm. Dust with powdered sugar.   Serves 8.

*A Late Harvest Zinfandel tends to be richer bodied, sweeter and more flavorful.

This cake goes very well with a Late Harvest Zinfandel.

Drunken Fruit Compote

1 ½ cups mixed dried fruit
¼ cup black raisins
¼ cup golden raisins
4 cups water
¼ cup whole peeled, toasted
 almonds
1 slice of lemon

¼ cup sugar
2 cinnamon sticks
¼ cup dry Sherry
¼ cup Sauvignon Blanc wine
½ cup fresh orange juice
1 cup fresh raspberries or
 blackberries (optional)

Bring all dried fruits and 2 cups of the water to a boil. Reduce heat, add almonds, lemon, sugar and the remaining 2 cups of water. Simmer 10 minutes. Remove from heat. Remove lemon slice.

Put in large bowl. Add cinnamon sticks, Sherry, wine and orange juice. Add fresh berries, if using.

Chill well. This is better the next day.   Makes 4 small desserts.

Serve with a white wine.

Blackberry Zinfandel Sherbet

2 pounds blackberries, rinsed
2 cups Zinfandel wine
½ cup sugar
½ teaspoon cracked black
 pepper

1 teaspoon grated fresh lemon
 zest
¼ cup Crème de Cassis
 liqueur
Juice of 1 lemon

In a saucepan, place blackberries, wine, sugar, pepper, lemon zest and Cassis. Bring to a boil. Turn down heat and cook slowly for 15 minutes. Remove from heat and cool to room temperature.

Sieve into a clean bowl. Add juice from 1 lemon; stir. Chill

Process in an ice cream freezer. Serve with toasted almonds.
                                                    Serves 4 to 6.

Serve with a well-chilled Zinfandel.

Poached Pears In Wine with Sauce

3 ½ cups Zinfandel wine
1 cinnamon stick
1 teaspoon fresh lemon
  juice

1 large strip lemon peel,
  halved lengthwise
4 firm ripe pears, peeled,
  cored and halved lengthwise

Bring wine, cinnamon, lemon juice and lemon peel to boil. Turn heat down and place pears in saucepan. Add water if necessary to cover tops of pears. Poach the pears on simmer until done, about 8 minutes. Remove the pears and cool. Simmer remaining liquid until it becomes a thick, sticky sauce.

To serve, fan the pears on plates. Top with sauce and vanilla ice cream. Accompany with ginger snaps.   Serves 4.

Serve with a Zinfandel.

A Compote of Country Fruit

⅓ cup Zinfandel wine
⅓ cup balsamic vinegar
2 tablespoons sugar
2 tablespoons strawberry
  preserves

2 cups strawberries
1 large red apple, peeled and
  cored
1 large orange, peeled
1 cup seedless grapes

Combine wine, vinegar, sugar and preserves and mix well. Cut strawberries in half. Cut apple and orange into the same size pieces as strawberries. Toss fruit with marinade. Chill for minimum of 2 hours, stirring every 20 minutes or so. Marinating overnight works best.

Serve with cookies, or over ice cream or pound cake.   Serves 8.

Serve with a Zinfandel.

Strawberries and Crème Fraîche Crepes
with Pinot Noir Sauce

A lot of work, but well worth the effort!

1 cup heavy whipping cream
½ cup buttermilk
¼ cup fresh orange juice
¼ cup grenadine
2 tablespoons Crème de
   Cassis liqueur
1 tablespoon Grande Marnier
   liqueur
1 ½ cups Pinot Noir wine

⅓ cup sugar
2 pints strawberries, stems
   removed and diced into ¼-
   inch cubes
1 tablespoon cornstarch
Brown sugar
Mint sprigs
Dessert Crepes (recipe
   follows)

To make the crème fraîche, combine the whipping cream and buttermilk and let sit at room temperature for 6 to 8 hours until it has thickened.

Place the next six ingredients in a saucepan and heat until the sugar dissolves. Allow to cool until tepid. Place strawberries in a mixing bowl and pour cooled liquid over them. Place in refrigerator and allow to stand for 4 hours.

Strain liquid back into saucepan and set strawberries aside in mixing bowl. Slowly whisk ¼ cup water into the cornstarch to make a slurry. Bring to a boil and slowly add the cornstarch slurry, stirring constantly until the mixture thickens. Remove the sauce from the heat and whisk over an ice bath until cool. Refrigerate until needed. Meanwhile, prepare Dessert Crepes

DESSERT CREPES:
½ cup water
1 ½ cup milk
1 to 2 teaspoons Grande
   Marnier liqueur or Brandy
4 large eggs

2 cups all-purpose flour
2 tablespoons sugar
Pinch of salt
3 tablespoons unsalted butter,
   melted

Blend liquids and eggs together with a whisk or in a blender. Slowly add flour, sugar, and salt and continue to whisk or blend until smooth.

Blend in melted butter and refrigerate for at least 30 minutes. The batter should be the consistency of heavy cream. If the batter is too thick add a little water.

Brush a crepe pan, or a 6 or 8-inch non-stick sauté pan, with a little clarified butter or oil after it has been heated over a moderate flame. The pan is hot enough when a drop of batter sizzles on the pan.

While rolling the pan, add around ¼ cup of the batter making a thin layer that covers the bottom of the pan. Cook until the sides of the crepe turn light brown and lift slightly from the surface of the pan. Flip using a thin rubber spatula and cook other side until brown. Remove and repeat the cooking process until batter is used up. Makes about 12 crepes.

Spread a thin layer of crème fraîche in the center part of a crepe. Sprinkle ½ teaspoon brown sugar; add ¼ cup strawberries and roll crepes. Place two crepes on a plate, pour sauce over and garnish with a dollop of crème fraîche and a sprig of mint.   Serves 6.

Serve with a Rosé Sparkling Wine or Champagne.

Brandy Pots de Crème

9 egg yolks	½ vanilla bean, scraped
⅓ cup sugar	⅔ cup chopped chocolate
3 cups cream	⅛ cup Brandy

Whisk egg yolks. Boil cream, sugar and vanilla bean. Strain. Pour ⅔ of the mixture into egg yolks, whisking well. Set aside.

Add chocolate to remaining ⅓ cream mixture, stirring until melted. Add Brandy. Ladle chocolate into custard cups, filling half full. Cover each with reserved vanilla mixture. Place custard cups in a baking pan to which you have added sufficient water to come half way up on the sides of the custard cups. Cover with foil and bake in a 325 degree oven for 35 to 40 minutes. Remove from oven and cool to room temperature. Wrap individually in foil or plastic and chill in refrigerator for 2 hours before serving.   Serves 8.

Serve with Champagne.

Champagne Sorbet

1 teaspoon egg white
1 teaspoon white corn syrup
⅛ teaspoon ground cardamom
3 cups Champagne

2 cups freshly squeezed
  orange juice
1 ¼ cups simple syrup (recipe
  follows)

Make simple syrup first.

SIMPLE SYRUP:
2 cups sugar   1 cup water

In a small saucepan, mix water and sugar, stirring to dissolve the sugar. Bring to a boil, remove from heat, and set aside to cool. Measure out 1 ¼ cups syrup, reserving remainder for another use.

In a mixing bowl, whisk together egg white, corn syrup and cardamom. Add Champagne, orange juice and simple syrup. Whip together well. Freeze in an ice cream machine according to manufacturer's directions.   Serves 10 to 12.

This light summer dessert is best when served with a chilled Champagne.

Sorbet of Gamay Beaujolais

3 ½ cups Gamay Beaujolais
   wine
2 tablespoons sugar
Pinch freshly ground black
   pepper

Pinch cinnamon
2 cups slightly mashed fresh
   berries (blackberries,
   raspberries, or a mixture)

Pour wine into a large steel or glass saucepan. Bring to a boil over high heat, then turn flame to low and let simmer for 10 minutes. (This process should remove most of the alcohol in the wine, allowing it to freeze successfully.) Allow to cool to room temperature.

Stir in sugar until completely dissolved. This sorbet is best when not too sweet, especially when used during a meal as an intermezzo. If served as a dessert, slightly more sweetness is acceptable.

Add black pepper and cinnamon to wine mixture and refrigerate 2 hours.

Freeze in an ice cream freezer according to manufacturer's directions. Add the berries just before the sorbet is finished and continue freezing until done. Serve immediately or store in airtight containers up to 2 months. Very pretty when served in wine glasses!
                    Makes approximately one quart.

Serve with a Gamay Beaujolais.

Pear Champagne Sorbet

5 pears, peeled, cored and cut
  into cubes
1 cup Champagne
2 tablespoons pear liqueur
¾ cup sugar

½ teaspoon freshly grated
  nutmeg
1 teaspoon lemon juice
½ cup heavy cream

Simmer all ingredients except cream in a saucepan until pears are soft and alcohol has evaporated, approximately 10 to 15 minutes. Blend until smooth in a food processor. Let mixture cool.

Add the heavy cream to pear mixture and mix thoroughly. Freeze in an ice cream maker according to manufacturers directions.

Serves 4 to 6.

Serve with Champagne.

Peach Wine Sorbet

6 to 7 large fresh peaches
Juice of 1 lemon
1 cup Sauvignon Blanc wine

½ cup honey
Peach slices for garnish
Mint sprigs for garnish

Peel and purée peaches to make 5 cups of purée.

Mix peach purée well with lemon, wine and honey. Freeze in ice cream maker according to manufacturers directions. Serve garnished with extra peach slices and mint sprigs.   Serves 8.

Serve with a Sauvignon Blanc.

Sparkling Sabayon with Cookies Florentine

7 large egg yolks	2 tablespoons Kirsch liqueur
½ cup sugar	Cookies Florentine (recipe
Pinch of salt	follows)
1 cup Champagne (Brut)	

Beat the yolks, sugar and salt until light. Place mixture in top of a double boiler and whisk in the Champagne and Kirsch. Place over simmering water and whisk until the mixture mounds and quadruples in volume.

Serve immediately (warm) with fresh fruits and berries and with Cookies Florentine.

COOKIES FLORENTINE:

½ cup butter	1 cup chopped walnuts
½ cup light corn syrup	½ cup flour
½ cup sugar	1 tablespoon grated lemon rind

Combine butter, corn syrup and sugar in a saucepan. Place over low heat, stirring frequently, until warm. Blend in walnuts and flour. Add lemon rind. Mix well.

On greased cookie sheet, make circles (4 inches in diameter) using approximately 2 tablespoons of dough per circle. Bake at 350 degrees for about 10 minutes or until golden brown. Cool slightly

Roll circles around the handle of wooden spoon to form tubes. Allow to cool completely and harden before serving.

Makes 8 servings.

Serve with Champagne.

Apricot Soufflé with Pear Sauce

2 cups sieved apricot jam,
  measured after sieving
2 tablespoons pear liqueur

12 egg whites
Pear Sauce (recipe follows)

Prepare twelve 6-ounce soufflé dishes by spraying them with vegetable oil and dusting with sugar.

Combine sieved jam and liqueur in a large bowl. Whisk until smooth. In a separate bowl, whisk the egg whites until they form peaks. Fold into the jam mixture just until combined. Spoon into the prepared soufflé dishes and level off the tops. (This may be done up to 1 hour ahead of baking. Keep refrigerated.) Meanwhile, prepare Pear Sauce.

PEAR SAUCE:
2 cups peeled and diced pears
¼ cup brown sugar
2 tablespoons pear liqueur
2 tablespoons water

1 teaspoon freshly grated
  nutmeg
⅛ teaspoon salt

Combine pears with other Ingredients in saucepan. Bring to a boil. Purée in a blender and strain through a fine sieve.

To bake soufflés, place on middle rack of a 350 degree oven and bake for 10 to 15 minutes. Remove and serve immediately with Pear Sauce.
      Serves 12.

Serve with Champagne.

Chocolate-Walnut Torte

2 cups whole shelled walnuts
6 ½ ounces unsweetened
  chocolate
7 egg yolks
1 cup sugar

½ cup plus 5 tablespoons
  unsalted butter, softened
2 tablespoons Brandy
Powdered sugar

Preheat the oven to 350 degrees.

Butter the bottom of an 8-inch springform pan and line with parchment paper. Lightly butter and flour the paper and the sides of the pan.

In a food processor or blender, grind walnuts and chocolate to a medium-fine consistency.

In a medium mixing bowl, beat egg yolks and sugar until light and fluffy. Add the softened butter, and beat until smooth.

Add the walnut-chocolate mixture and the Brandy. Beat until well blended, 2 to 3 minutes. The batter will be very dense; scrape it into the prepared pan.

Bake the cake in the lower third of the oven for 45 minutes, or until a skewer inserted in the center emerges clean.

Let the cake cool in the pan for 5 minutes. Remove from the pan and place on a serving plate. Let cool completely. Just before serving, sift powdered sugar oven the top.   Serves 8

A Cabernet Sauvignon will make a perfect accompaniment to this rich, dense cake.

Pairing Wine with Food

COOKING WITH WINE

Here are some suggestions on pairing wine with food. Please keep in mind that these are suggestions, not rules. While we have suggested many different wines to go with many different dishes, this does not mean that you must have five different wines for a five course meal. Many of these dishes such as appetizers, soups, entrées and desserts are often served separately. When you do, these are the wines we suggest.

The best suggestion is to serve the wine that goes with your main course or entrée for the entire meal. You may prefer a light wine before the meal and a sweet wine with dessert. But you can stay with the wine that pairs with your entrée for all your courses.

BEFORE THE MEAL

Champagne* (Brut), Chablis, Chenin Blanc, Reisling, French Columbard, Sauvignon Blanc, Gewürztraminer, Sémillon.

APPETIZERS & LIGHT FOODS

Antipasto . . . . Chenin Blanc, Chardonnay
Caviar . . . . Champagne (Brut)
Cheese, Soft & Creamy . . . . Chardonnay, Pinot Noir, Merlot
Charcuterie . . . . Pinot Noir, Merlot, Burgundy
Cheese, Cheddar and Hard . . . . Pinot Noir, Merlot
Cheese Fondue . . . . Reisling, Pinot Gris, Chardonnay
Crudities . . . . Zinfandel, Rosé, Cabernet Sauvignon
Escargot . . . . Pinot Blanc, Gewürztraminer, Zinfandel
Pâtés
  Vegetable and Poultry .Sauterne, White Zinfandel, Chardonnay
  Beef and Pork . . . . Pinot Noir, Reisling, Fumé Blanc
  Chicken and Goose Liver. . Gewürztraminer, Sémillon, Zinfandel
Prosciutto, with Fruit . . . Reisling, Gewürztraminer, Chardonnay
Quiche . . . . Sauvignon Blanc, Fumé Blanc, Pinot Gris
Smoked Salmon . . . . Champagne (Brut), Pinot Gris
Oysters . . . . Champagne (Brut) Chablis, Muscadet

SOUPS

Bisques . . . . Chardonnay, Chenin Blanc, Sauvignon Blanc
Clam Chowder . . . . Chardonnay, Pinot Gris, Dry Sauterne
Consomme . . . . Chardonnay, White Zinfandel, Dry Sherry
Cream Soups . . . . Chardonnay, Reisling
French Onion Soup . . . . Pinot Noir, Merlot, Cabernet Sauvignon
Bean Soup . . . . Sémillon, Reisling
Seafood Bisque . . . . Sauvignon Blanc, Fumé Blanc
Minestrone . . . . Pinot Noir, Cabernet Sauvignon, Grignolino
Chicken or Turkey Soup . . . . . . Chenin Blanc, Reisling, Gamay
Vichyssoise . . . . Sémillon, Reisling, Chardonnay

*"Champagne" and "Sparkling Wine" are used interchangeably in most of the United States. The most commonly available are: "Brut" which is the driest and most popular, "Extra Sec" or "Extra Dry" which is a bit sweeter, and "Sec" or "Dry" which is very sweet.

SALADS

(Note: Vinegar salad dressings are incompatible with wine. Use wine or lemon in salad dressings when serving wine with salad.)

Caesar Salad . . .   Sauvignon Blanc, Chenin Blanc, Chardonnay
Chicken Salad . . . . Sauvignon Blanc, Chenin Blanc
Lobster Salad . . . . Champagne (Brut), Reisling
Nicoise Salad . . . . . . Zinfandel, Chenin Blanc, Sauvignon Blanc
Crab or Shrimp Louis. . Reisling, Sauvignon Blanc, Chenin Blanc

BEEF

Barbecue Beef . . . . Chianti, Zinfandel, Petit Syrah
Steak or Prime Rib . . . . Pinot Noir, Merlot, Cabernet Sauvignon
Beef Capriccio . . . . Chardonnay, Burgundy, Pinot Noir
Beef Stew . . . . Pinot Noir, Cabernet Sauvignon, Merlot
Boiled Beef . . . . Pinot Noir, Merlot, Chardonnay
Beef Stroganoff . . . . Zinfandel, Chardonnay, Chenin Blanc
Hamburger . . . . Beaujolais, Chianti, Burgundy
Meat Loaf . . . . Zinfandel, Gewürztraminer, Merlot
Roast Beef . . . . Cabernet Sauvignon, Merlot, Pinot Noir
Corned Beef Hash . . . . Zinfandel, Barbera, Chianti
Oxtail (Osso Bucco) . . . . Chianti, Cabernet, Reisling

LAMB

Roast Lamb . . . . Cabernet Sauvignon, Pinot Noir
Barbecued Lamb . . White or Blush Zinfandel, Merlot, Pinot Noir
Lamb Curry . . . . Chardonnay, Sauvignon Blanc
Lamb Stew . . . . Cabernet Sauvignon, Pinot Noir
Mixed Grill . . . . Cabernet, Chianti, Burgundy
Moussaka . . . . Burgundy, Chianti, Merlot

PORK

Baked Ham . . . . Pinot Noir, Burgundy, Gewürztraminer
Roast Pork . . . . Rosé, Chenin Blanc, Chardonnay
Pork Chops . . . . Chardonnay, Pinot Noir, Merlot
Grilled Pork Tenderloin . . . . Pinot Noir, Cabernet Sauvignon
Barbecued Spareribs . . . White or Blush Zinfandel, Petite Syrah

VEAL

Calves Liver . . . . Merlot, Zinfandel, Pinot Noir
Roast Veal . . . . Merlot, Pinot Noir, Cabernet Sauvignon
Sweetbreads . . . . Reisling, Chardonnay, Gewürztraminer
Veal Chops . . . . Pinot Noir, Merlot, Cabernet Sauvignon
Wiener Schnitzel . . . . Reisling, Gewürztraminer

CHICKEN

Broiled or Roast Chicken . . . . . Chenin Blanc, Merlot, Zinfandel
Fried Chicken . . . . Chardonnay, Pinot Noir, Merlot
Baked Chicken . . . . Chardonnay, Sauvignon Blanc
Chicken Pot Pie . . . . Cabernet Sauvignon, Chardonnay, Merlot
Coq Au Vin . . . . Merlot, Cabernet Sauvignon, Pinot Noir
Chicken Cacciatore . . . . Barbera, Cabernet Sauvignon
Chicken Teriyaki . . . . . Zinfandel, Chardonnay, Sauvignon Blanc
Barbecued Chicken . . . Zinfandel, Merlot, Cabernet Sauvignon

POULTRY, MISC

Roast Cornish Hens . . . Merlot, Pinot Noir, Cabernet Sauvignon
Roast Duck . . . . Pinot Noir, Merlot, Cabernet Sauvignon
Roast Goose . . . . Pinot Noir, Barbera, Burgundy
Roast Turkey . . . . Chenin Blanc, Reisling, Pinot Noir, Zinfandel

SEAFOOD

Abalone . . . . Chardonnay, Sauvignon Blanc, Pinot Noir
Cod, Rock or Ling . . . . Sémillon, Chardonnay
Flounder . . . . Sauvignon Blanc, Chenin Blanc, Chardonnay
Haddock . . . . Chardonnay, Sauvignon Blanc
Halibut . . . . Chardonnay, Sauvignon Blanc
Perch . . . . Reisling, Chenin Blanc
Red Snapper . . . . Sauvignon Blanc, Pinot Gris, Rosé
Broiled Salmon . . . . Chardonnay, Reisling, Pinot Noir
Sea Bass . . . . Pinot Gris, Sémillon
Fillet of Sole Amandine . . . . Sauvignon Blanc, Chardonnay
Dover (Petrale) Sole . . . . Zinfandel, Sauvignon Blanc
Swordfish . . . . Pinot Noir, Cabernet Sauvignon
Trout . . . . Chardonnay, Sémillon
Grilled Tuna . . . . Chardonnay, Pinot Noir, Rosé
Bouillabaisse . . . . Pinot Noir, Cabernet Sauvignon

Cioppino . . . . Barbera, Cabernet Sauvignon, Zinfandel
Clam Chowder, New England Style . . . . Chardonnay, Pinot Gris
Clam Chowder, Manhattan Style . . . . Merlot, Pinot Noir
Fried Fish . . . . Sauvignon Blanc, Chardonnay, Pinot Noir
Crabs, Broiled or Steamed . . . . . Chardonnay, Sauvignon Blanc
Lobster, Broiled or Steamed . . . . Chardonnay, Champagne
Lobster Newburg . . . . Chardonnay, Chenin Blanc
Oysters on Half Shell . . . . Champagne (Brut), Chardonnay
Oysters, Cooked . . . . Chardonnay, Sémillon, Reisling
Oyster Stew . . . . Chardonnay, Fumé Blanc, Sémillon
Scallops . . . . Gewürztraminer, Chenin Blanc, Reisling
Shrimp, Cooked . . . . Chardonnay, Sauvignon Blanc

PASTA

With Meat/Tomato Sauce . . . . Merlot, Barbera, Zinfandel
With Cheese or Cream Sauce . . Chardonnay, Sémillon, Reisling
With Pesto Sauce (Basil) . . . . Sauvignon Blanc, Barbera

FOREIGN FOODS

Chinese
Vegetables, Steamed . . . . Gewürztraminer, Zinfandel
Chicken and Beef, Fried . . . . . Pinot Noir, Cabernet Sauvignon
Szechwan Cuisine . . . . Fumé Blanc, Chenin Blanc

Japanese
Sushi and Sashimi . . . . Sauvignon Blanc, Chenin Blanc
Seafood Dishes . . . . Sauvignon Blanc, Chenin Blanc
Teriyaki . . . . Pinot Noir, Cabernet Sauvignon, Merlot
Sukiyaki . . . . Zinfandel, Chenin Blanc

Thai
Mildly Spiced . . . . Chenin Blanc, Reisling
Very Spiced . . . . Chardonnay, Chenin Blanc
Poultry . . . . Pinot Noir, Cabernet Sauvignon

Mexican
Fajitas, Burritos, etc., Highly Spiced . . . Zinfandel, Petite Syrah
Enchiladas, Tamales . . . . Chardonnay, Chenin Blanc
Guacamole . . . . Chardonnay, Chenin Blanc, Fumé Blanc

Greek
Vegetable Dishes . . . . Sauvignon Blanc, Chenin Blanc
Lamb Dishes . . . . Pinot Noir, Cabernet Sauvignon
Couscous . . . . Zinfandel,.Rosé Pinot Noir
Misc.
Jambalaya . . . . Zinfandel, Petite Syrah, Chenin Blanc
Tandoori Chicken . . . . Sauvignon Blanc, Pinot Noir, Merlot
Paella . . . . Merlot, Sauvignon Blanc, Rosé
Indian Curries . . . . Chenin Blanc, Gewürztraminer, Petit Syrah

FAST FOODS

Frankfurters, Cold Cuts, etc. . . . Pinot Noir, Cabernet Sauvignon
Hamburger . . . . Beaujolais, Chianti, Burgundy
Pizza, without Meat . . . . Zinfandel, Petit Syrah, Chianti
Pizza, with Meat . . . . . Cabernet Sauvignon, Pinot Noir, Chianti
Fish and Chips . . . . Chablis, Sauvignon Blanc, Reisling
Chile Con Carne . . . . Barbera, Beaujolais, Zinfandel

DESSERTS

Chocolate
Cakes and Pies . . . . . . Muscat, Tawny Port, Pink Champagne
Mousses and Puddings . . Muscat, Chardonnay, Cream Sherry
Fruit Filled Pies and Tarts . . . . Reisling, Chardonnay, Zinfandel
Cakes, White, Angel, Etc. . . . . Cream or Oloroso Sherry
Cheesecake . . . . Zinfandel, Gewürztraminer
Crepes Suzette . . . . Champagne (Demi-Sec), Asti Spumante
Crème Brûlée . . . . Sauterne, Rhine, Muscadet
Fresh Fruit . . . . Chardonnay, Gewürztraminer, Reisling
Fruitcake . . . . Tawny Port, Cream Sherry

PERSONAL PAIRINGS

This is where you can record your personal pairing of wines to your own recipes, or to the ones in this cookbook. It is the best way to select the right wine to go with what you are serving. And, if you really don't like one that you've tried, make a note of it. There's no sense in making the same mistake twice, it there?

The Wine   **The Recipes**

Brand_____ _____
Type_____ _____
Vintage_____ _____
Reserve_____ _____
Estate_____ _____
Appellation_____ _____
Notes_____ _____

The Wine   **The Recipes**

Brand_____ _____
Type_____ _____
Vintage_____ _____
Reserve_____ _____
Estate_____ _____
Appellation_____ _____
Notes_____ _____

The Wine   **The Recipes**

Brand_____ _____
Type_____ _____
Vintage_____ _____
Reserve_____ _____
Estate_____ _____
Appellation_____ _____
Notes_____ _____

Personal Pairings

The Wine

Brand_____

Type_____

Vintage_____

Reserve_____

Estate_____

Appellation_____

Notes_____

The Recipes

_____

_____

_____

_____

_____

_____

_____

The Wine

Brand_____

Type_____

Vintage_____

Reserve_____

Estate_____

Appellation_____

Notes_____

The Recipes

_____

_____

_____

_____

_____

_____

_____

The Wine

Brand_____

Type_____

Vintage_____

Reserve_____

Estate_____

Appellation_____

Notes_____

The Recipes

_____

_____

_____

_____

_____

_____

_____

The Wine

Brand_____

Type_____

Vintage_____

Reserve_____

Estate_____

Appellation_____

Notes_____

The Recipes

_____

_____

_____

_____

_____

_____

_____

The Wine

Brand_____

Type_____

Vintage_____

Reserve_____

Estate_____

Appellation_____

Notes_____

The Recipes

_____

_____

_____

_____

_____

_____

_____

The Wine

Brand_____

Type_____

Vintage_____

Reserve_____

Estate_____

Appellation_____

Notes_____

The Recipes

_____

_____

_____

_____

_____

_____

_____

The Wine

Brand_____

Type_____

Vintage_____

Reserve_____

Estate_____

Appellation_____

Notes_____

The Recipes

_____

_____

_____

_____

_____

_____

_____

The Wine

Brand_____

Type_____

Vintage_____

Reserve_____

Estate_____

Appellation_____

Notes_____

The Recipes

_____

_____

_____

_____

_____

_____

_____

Personal Pairings

The Wine

Brand_____

Type_____

Vintage_____

Reserve_____

Estate_____

Appellation_____

Notes_____

The Recipes

_____

_____

_____

_____

_____

_____

_____

The Wine

Brand_____

Type_____

Vintage_____

Reserve_____

Estate_____

Appellation_____

Notes_____

The Recipes

_____

_____

_____

_____

_____

_____

_____

The Wine

Brand_____

Type_____

Vintage_____

Reserve_____

Estate_____

Appellation_____

Notes_____

The Recipes

_____

_____

_____

_____

_____

_____

_____

The Wine

Brand_____

Type_____

Vintage_____

Reserve_____

Estate_____

Appellation_____

Notes_____

The Recipes

_____

_____

_____

_____

_____

_____

_____

Index

COOKING WITH WINE

Index

POSTSCRIPT

If your book, gift or gourmet store does not have these other books of ours, you may order them by phone, fax, or mail. Your money back if you are not delighted.

"Cooking With Wine" . . . . $14.95 plus $3.00 S&H

"The Great Little Food With Wine Book", includes 76 recipes by some of America's finest winery chefs. Here, too, are simple and easy to follow guides on how and where to buy wine, how to decipher the wine menu in a restaurant, and pairing your favorite foods with wine . . . . $7.95 plus $2.00 S&H

"The California Wine Country Cookbook II", a collection of 172 favorite recipes by 102 chefs of The California Wine Country. There's a section on cooking with wine and a brief history of wine in California . . . . $12.95 plus $3.00 S&H

"The California Wine Country Herbs & Spices Cookbook", a collection of 188 recipes by 72 chefs, winemakers, and wineries featuring herbs and spices. Included are recipes for making herbed oils and vinegars, and spice mixes, and the romantic history of the spices . . . . . $12.95 plus $3.00 S&H

TO ORDER (24 hours a day): Call toll free (800) 852-4890 or Fax (707) 538-7371. Hoffman Press, P.O. Box 2996, Santa Rosa, CA 95405-2996.